Engines of Innovation

Holden Thorp & Buck Goldstein

Engines of

Innovation

The Entrepreneurial University in the Twenty-First Century

SECOND EDITION
With a new preface and
chapter by the authors

THE UNIVERSITY OF
NORTH CAROLINA PRESS
Chapel Hill

This book was
published with
the assistance
of the William R.
Kenan Jr. Fund
of the University
of North Carolina
Press.

© 2010 Holden Thorp and Buck Goldstein
"Preface to the Second Edition" and "Engines Revisited—A
Three-Year Tune-Up" © 2013 Holden Thorp and Buck Goldstein

All royalties from this book have been assigned by
the authors to the University of North Carolina at
Chapel Hill to support innovation and entrepreneurship.

Designed by Richard Hendel
Set in Arnhem and Fedra types
by Tseng Information Systems, Inc.
Manufactured in the United States of America

The paper in this book meets the guidelines for permanence and
durability of the Committee on Production Guidelines for Book
Longevity of the Council on Library Resources.

The University of North Carolina Press has been a member
of the Green Press Initiative since 2003.

The Library of Congress has cataloged the
original edition of this book as follows:
Thorp, H. Holden, 1964–
Engines of innovation : the entrepreneurial university in the
twenty-first century / Holden Thorp and Buck Goldstein
    p. cm.
Includes bibliographical references and index.
1. Community and college—United States. 2. Education,
Higher—Aims and objectives—United States. 3. Business and
education—United States. 4. Entrepreneurship—United States.
I. Thorp, H. Holden. II. Goldstein, Buck.
LC238.T46 2010
378.1'03 22   2010018135

ISBN 978-1-4696-0984-3 (pbk.: alk. paper)
ISBN 978-1-4696-1184-6 (e-book)
ISBN 978-0-8078-3438-1 (cloth: alk. paper) (2010)

17 16 15 14 13   5 4 3 2 1

For the latest on the authors and their work with innovation and
higher education go to www.innovationandeducation.com.

For Patti and Kay

Contents

The proverb "be careful what you wish for" applies to the events that followed the publication of the first edition of *Engines of Innovation*. It was our hope that a worldwide economic crisis would become an opportunity too important to miss and would give rise to innovative approaches to the world's biggest problems, with America's research universities leading the way in finding solutions. We got much more than we bargained for. The meltdown was not merely a financial event but rather a fundamental challenge to the most basic assumptions about our society and the institutions that anchor it. Geopolitical alignments such as the European Union have been tested by economic realities whose resolution had long been postponed. Repressive political regimes were confronted and in some instances toppled by democratic movements aided by social media. The very existence of many of the world's largest corporations and financial institutions has been challenged, and in many cases their underlying economic models are in question. Grassroots, citizen-led movements challenging the status quo exist in virtually every major country, including our own, increasing instability throughout the world.

Research universities have not been exempt from the turmoil. The initial shock of eroded endowments was followed by substantial cuts in governmental support, especially for state-supported universities, requiring cost-cutting responses that ranged from the enactment of much-needed efficiencies to draconian cuts in faculty numbers and compensation that threaten the long-term viability of state-supported research universities. With the restoration of a degree of financial stability, at least for research universities, it has become clear that a new normal has taken shape, in which, as we predicted in the first edition of *Engines*, students, faculty, parents, trustees, state and federal government, and the public at large all expect more from institutions often referred to as the crown jewels of our society. The often-contradictory demands from these diverse constituencies include questioning the value of tenure for faculty, preparing students more effectively for the job market, increasing the graduation rate among enrolled students and the number of college graduates overall, reducing the cost of higher education and the taxpayers' role in financing it, reducing need-based financial aid, reforming intercollegiate athletics, and providing an array of alternatives to the residential college experience that remains the principal educational model among American research universities. Some opinion makers have also begun to question the value of a college education, pointing to Bill Gates, Steve Jobs, and others as examples of college dropouts who achieved enormous success. These debates often ignore the high costs of not getting a college degree and the even higher costs of starting and not finishing one.

So the financial crisis that served as a touchstone for the introduction to the first edition of *Engines* has now given way to four forces that are shaping higher education. First, online education, about which we will say more below and in the new closing chapter, has become a constant topic in trustee meetings and in the punditry. Second, student debt has taken on increased attention in light of questions about the value of college education and its costs. Third, health care reform poses a set of challenges for research universities with large medical centers. Finally, the U.S. fiscal situation has created uncertainties around research funding and federal financial aid. These four forces must be turned into opportunities for advancement, and we believe the entrepreneurial thinking we propose points the way for doing so.

The response to our ideas both on our own campus and among our peers nationwide has been more rapid and more dramatic than we expected. Our own experience with an outside consulting firm helping us find efficiencies among activities not directly connected to our academic mission has now been replicated at scores of educational institutions both big and small. This will be a long and sometimes painful process that should be ongoing, just as it is in any successful institution, governmental agency, or corporation. More significantly, reductions in funds, especially for state-supported universities, combined with advances in online technology and social media and the worldwide demand for American higher education, has spawned a remarkable array of online models for delivering knowledge to a large number of students. With experience, the effectiveness of these models will increase and revenue streams will be developed, so that online education in general and, more specifically, the new MOOCs (Massive Open Online Courses) will change the basic curriculum in all of higher education, with research universities leading the way. Again, the hard work of perfecting the existing models and inventing new ones will be slower than the initial burst of innovation we have experienced over the last eighteen months, but the results, we believe, will be positive, as technology is employed to transfer knowledge not only more efficiently but also more effectively.

Other responses are not so positive. Governors, state legislatures, and commissions appointed by governmental authorities across the country are, in the name of financial austerity, attempting to drastically diminish institutions that have taken decades or even centuries to build. Many believe that the state-supported public research university will cease to exist in its current form and will be replaced by a hybrid model that relies more on tuition and federal grant money and dramatically less on state funds. More fundamentally, many of the ideals of the modern university, particularly those grounded in the study of the liberal arts and humanities, are being called into question in the name of practicality. An increasingly familiar refrain from parents, legislators, and the public at large is, "How will studying English help a student get a job?" Such concerns are particularly compelling when unemployment among recent college graduates is estimated by some to be as high as 50 percent. We believe the critics exaggerate the unemployment numbers and underestimate the long-term quantitative benefits of a college education. But we are mindful of the fact that a grand vision of the research university as a crown jewel of our society has much less resonance when its graduates are beating the pavement in search of that all-important first job.

Based on our observations and hundreds of conversations with others, however, we believe the fundamental ideas expressed in *Engines of Innovation* continue to provide a blueprint for increasing the impact of our great research universities. First, our own experience demonstrates that culture trumps structure when attempting to make a university more entrepreneurial. Beginning in 2010, at the University of North Carolina at Chapel Hill we began pursuing an innovation road map, Innovate@Carolina, that has resulted in literally hundreds of initiatives in every corner of the institution, including the adoption of a campus-wide theme to address the worldwide problem of clean water, a seed capital fund for innovative projects in the humanities, and a large survey course on innovation and entrepreneurship open to anyone in the university and taught by the two of us. All of this was done without the creation of a new department, center, institute, or analogous administrative structure. We did have an energetic and experienced person serving as special assistant to the chancellor for innovation, together with some part-time staff, to chronicle our progress, connect some dots, and provide mostly moral support. As of this writing, we have raised over $70 million in support of the vision embodied in Innovate@Carolina but without the overhead and politics associated with a new academic entity.

Second, our conviction that virtually nothing important will get done in our great universities without the involvement of problem-based, multidisciplinary teams is stronger than ever. Our conviction was solidified by the work on our own campus of a strategic planning group chaired by Chancellor Emeritus James Moeser that involved deans, vice-chancellors, department chairs, and even the athletic director and the director of admissions. Each engaged in a yearlong planning process, the results of which were shared with the other members of Chancellor Moeser's group and ultimately with the Board of Trustees of the university. By the end of the second yearlong cycle there has yet to be a final plan that was not multidisciplinary, and almost uniformly the aspiration of the leaders involved is to increase the level of cooperation both across campus and with organizations and individuals outside of academia. Similarly, the newly created Water Institute in the School of Public Health is a problem-based, multidisciplinary research effort that serves as a model for implementing much of what we have written on interdisciplinarity.

Third, if anything, we underestimated the importance of social entrepreneurship in winning the hearts and minds of the academic community and making a difference in the world. At a campus-wide symposium moderated by the chair of the History Department, time and again unlikely attendees, primarily from the arts and humanities, made clear the fact that they were engaged because the idea of social entrepreneurship was appealing to them and offered a comfortable "front porch" for entrepreneurial ideas they might otherwise find objectionable. Similarly, our Campus Y, a voice for social justice at UNC for more than 150 years, has embraced social entrepreneurship as central to its mission and has established in its building a social innovation incubator, where the university's first social entrepreneur in residence presides over, among other things, capacity-building workshops for the social sector.

Continuing conversations about other chapters in *Engines* confirm that our basic ideas have merit others can appreciate. Not surprisingly, our critics continue, with great passion, to highlight what they see as serious flaws in our reasoning. However, the past two years have made clear to us something we didn't expect. We underestimated the challenge of bringing excellent execution, the day-to-day blocking and tackling required to make any idea a reality, to an academic environment that is essentially a group of independent contractors, each with a diverse set of constituents and demands. The challenge manifested itself in many ways. In our faculty boot camp, which we discuss in Chapter 7, we learned that many senior colleagues had no training in activities such as structuring a productive staff meeting or developing a set of measurable goals and the metrics required to track them. Providing such training was easy to do and yielded immediate positive results. We also learned that the infrastructure that supported virtually every aspect of the university was outmoded and incapable of providing the data or supervision required by any twenty-first-century enterprise. This surfaced as we attempted to identify cost savings in simple areas such as procurement, travel, and information technology. The increased accountability that all universities will confront and which we discuss in Chapter 10 will make improved infrastructure and information technology a challenging issue for all of us in the next several years.

Finally, one of us decided to make a career change, when Holden Thorp moved from being chancellor at UNC-Chapel Hill to provost at Washington University in St. Louis. The great public research universities of America are striking symbols of the promise of democracy, the vision of our nation's founders, and the courage of the legislators who passed the Morrill Act in 1862, whose foresight produced institutions that perform three-quarters of the federal research and grant three-quarters of the graduate and professional degrees in the nation—all while charging deeply discounted tuitions that promote accessibility. But, as Hunter Rawlings, president of the American Association of Universities, discussed in a talk on our campus, five forces are currently challenging the foundations of public higher education in America: strain on state budgets due to Medicaid, system-flagship conflict, ideological differences, institutional complexity, and intercollegiate athletics. These challenges have played out—in some cases with great fireworks—at numerous public flagships, including UNC-Chapel Hill, in recent years. The personal transition of one of us from a public institution to a private one does not lessen our conviction that the entrepreneurial thinking we advocate in *Engines* is critical as public universities are being asked to make the case for their very existence, and it reinforces the idea that innovation and entrepreneurship are equally important in the private sphere as universities are called upon to use their vast financial and human resources to address the critical needs of the nation and the world.

Clearly, the journey continues. We will discuss in the final chapter of this second edition developments that have taken place in the last several years, but the pace of change in higher education is accelerating beyond our most aggressive expectations. Rather than writing another book discussing this change, we have decided to participate in it by continuing the dialogue with our colleagues around the country and the world and by engaging in the new models for teaching and learning that are emerging almost daily. There are few opportunities as exciting and as daunting as the current transformation of higher education. We consider ourselves fortunate to find that we are in the middle of a revolution not of our making but in which we are now enthusiastic participants.

Engines of Innovation

Introduction

We are not the first authors to be halfway through writing a book when the world changed. True, in the fall of 2008, Newtonian laws were not repealed (that took place during the Internet bubble), nor was a conclusive proof of Einstein's general theory of relativity advanced. Still, the world experienced the greatest financial crisis since the Great Depression with trillions of dollars of wealth wiped out in a matter of weeks and the viability of a highly complex and interdependent global financial system severely tested. Of course, the airwaves and cyberspace were filled with commentary on the causes of the crisis. The two of us were highly interested observers in all of this, especially because one of us was leading a major research university and the other was teaching a group of 100 entrepreneurs and advising three high-tech companies. Yet aside from comments on the reduced size of university endowments we did not believe the economic crisis would have a major impact on this book.

Two individuals we admire caused us to reconsider. First, as part of a panel on the world economic crisis, Eric Schmidt, CEO of Google, said, "We are going to have to innovate our way out of this thing and our great research universities will have to lead the way."[1] A week later, Harvard's world-renowned strategist, Michael Porter, declared that America urgently needs a coherent economic strategy based in large part upon our strengths in innovation, entrepreneurship, and higher education.[2] Their comments helped us crystallize a conviction we intuitively understood but had yet to articulate. No longer were we writing a book aimed primarily at university presidents, boards of trustees, and philanthropists interested in increasing the impact of the work that goes on at the nation's leading research universities. Instead, we were writing about the critical role of research universities in helping reshape America and the world—not solely in terms of the economy, but also in addressing other grand challenges. If, as Rahm Emanuel, President Obama's chief of staff, reminded us, "You never want a serious crisis to go to waste," then universities, as engines of innovation, have a major responsibility.[3]

For one of us, the world changed in a more personal way as well. After only a year as dean of the College of Arts and Sciences at the University of North Carolina at Chapel Hill, Holden Thorp became the tenth chancellor of the university and, at forty-three, one of its youngest. Chancellors typically write books at the end of their terms, not the beginning. That way, the prospect of failing to meet meticulously outlined expectations is eliminated. On the other hand, laying out a vision for the university as an engine for innovation invites real accountability. Results are measured against rhetoric. Moreover, being chancellor takes an enormous amount of time, leaving room for little else. We discussed all of this and decided to press on. Not only did the times make our book all the more important, but now one of us had to discern how our thinking should be applied to our own institution.

Once the dust cleared and we had a chance to think about the Schmidt sound bite and the Porter article, three themes emerged. Fortunately they are intertwined with the ideas that motivated us to write this book in the first place. First, innovation has to be central to any meaningful response to global crises—economic and otherwise. A new economy cannot be rebuilt by replicating the New Deal. In the future, the buildings housing those who will create well-paying, sustainable jobs, and provide the United States with a sustainable competitive advantage in the global economy, are not courthouses or government offices but research labs, classrooms, and innovation centers where big ideas are hatched and subsequently translated into reality. The superhighways that will change the world are not asphalt but electronic, and rather than connecting the world's great cities the new superhighways provide access to most of the world's knowledge. What is most exciting about innovation is that it begins with a problem; the bigger the problem, the more significant the innovation needed. From the very beginning of our work, we have been convinced that for research universities to realize their full potential, they must attack the world's biggest problems, and this notion is increasingly being embraced throughout academia.

Attacking the world's biggest problems—problems such as hunger, the shortage of water, climate change, and inequality—serves as an ideal organizing principle that will encourage a multitude of large and small innovations. The long-term impact of such innovation on the economy is almost incalculable. For instance, the amount of activity spawned by the Internet is well known. But the Internet is simply the latest chapter in a long history of often-simple innovations leading to enormous economic activity. The light bulb, the Model T, and the container ship lead a parade of American innovations that have profoundly changed the world. As Professor Porter points out, the United States has been uniquely good at turning research into innovation and turning that innovation into commercial activity.[4] Over half the patents filed worldwide come from the United States. From a historical perspective, it would be safe to say that innovation has been one of America's core competencies, and if innovation is to be a primary engine of world economic growth, the United States has a central role to play. The most important point about innovation and academia is that maximum impact occurs in response to a problem. Problem-based innovation in research universities can focus resources from a variety of disciplines on the challenges we face and, in so doing, create new knowledge and economic growth.

The second theme that emerges from Schmidt's and Porter's comments is that the nation's research universities are expected by those who support them and the public at large to lead the way as far as innovation is concerned. In his *Business Week* article, Porter characterizes U.S. universities as the best in the world, as magnets for global talent, as engines for innovation and commercial development. Federal and state governments have invested billions annually for research and teaching, and private donors have made modern American research universities among the best-endowed institutions in our society. A vast majority of all Nobel Prize winners were either educated by or teach at American research universities. It is estimated that two-thirds to three-quarters of the best universities in the world are in the United States—a claim that could be made for few other institutions in our country.[5]

Now more than ever, funding sources and other supporters are looking for a measurable return on their investment. It is no longer merely desirable for universities to be the source of innovations. It is now a national priority. Institutions that have received so much over the years—and that are generally perceived as one of the crown jewels of American culture—must now step up at a time of crisis and play a central role in addressing pressing issues facing the world.

It should not be surprising that the university is thrust in this role. As Peter Drucker, the leading thinker on innovation and entrepreneurship in the twentieth century, explains, the creation of the modern research university was itself an entrepreneurial act.[6] German diplomat Wilhelm von Humboldt founded the University of Berlin in 1809 as an institution of change. It was created to wrest intellectual and scientific leadership from the French and to capture the innovative energy that resulted from the tremendous economic and cultural upheaval precipitated by the French Revolution. In the United States, following the passage of the Morrill Act in 1862, Cornell University was founded in 1865 as our first modern research university. Cornell was the result of a partnership between an academic, Andrew D. White, and an entrepreneur, Ezra Cornell, the founder of Western Union. The new university emphasized the teaching of "practical subjects" as well as research that would lead to progress and the betterment of society.[7] Soon after, in 1876, a second such partnership between Johns Hopkins, a railroad man, and Daniel Coit Gilman, an academic, resulted in the creation of Johns Hopkins University, with the mission of supporting the world's great scholars in their efforts to advance knowledge for the betterment of mankind. By the end of the century, two more models for innovative research and education emerged. The University of Chicago was created by John D. Rockefeller and William Rainey Harper for the purpose of spreading "useful knowledge." Stanford University was established by Leland Stanford, another railroad man, to help young people undertake a "useful life." In Drucker's words, there is no better text for a history of innovation and entrepreneurship than the creation of the modern university, and especially the modern American research university.[8]

There is another reason the experts and the public at large look to research universities in a time of crisis: all the pieces are in place. It is estimated that the combined endowments of America's top 125 research universities exceed $250 billion dollars. These institutions also command more than 70 percent of university science and research space and account for almost 80 percent of all research and development expenditures. But more important than the enormous financial resources the top research universities control is the broad-based research and teaching infrastructure they have built not only in the sciences and the professional schools but in the liberal arts. These top universities grant three-quarters of all Ph.D.s and over a third of all professional degrees in the United States.[9] It is this human capital — the heart and soul of these institutions — that can and must drive a culture of innovation. If Eric Schmidt is correct and we are going to have to innovate our way out of the current crisis, the most important factor in achieving this goal is the people referred to by the noted social critic Richard Florida as the "creative class."[10] These scientists, artists, poets, designers, computer programmers, venture capitalists, and entrepreneurs have skill sets that allow them to live almost anywhere, but for a variety of economic and cultural reasons they migrate to academic hubs such as Silicon Valley; Route 128 near Boston; the Research Triangle Park in North Carolina; Austin, Texas; Ann Arbor, Michigan; and San Diego, California, to name just a few. Together, these hubs form an ecosystem that is, in effect, a social structure for innovation. How and why these innovation hubs come into being is Florida's interest; ours is the fact that they form around research universities, that they are incredibly diverse, and that they are in place and ready to go.

Not only are the people in place, but universities, as hubs of creativity, are the keepers of an enduring culture of innovation that is unique among the world's great institutions. If you wonder about their resiliency, consider the following: of the eighty-five institutions in existence since 1522 — the Catholic Church and Britain's Parliament among them — seventy are universities.[11] The remarkable endurance of institutions of higher learning is due to their adherence to founding principles. The original mission began as early as 1088 with the founding of the University of Bologna and its express purpose of promulgating research independent of any other power. Universities have honed a culture of creativity independent of other social institutions — a remarkable and enviable achievement. But now the bill has come due for all the resources and freedom bestowed upon our universities. The great gifts our civilization has given to its most elite institutions must now be called upon. The remarkable culture created centuries ago to produce innovation by gathering in one place great minds from across the disciplines is again expected to provide the next big ideas that will transform society.

The final theme suggested by Schmidt's and Porter's commentaries is clearly the most problematic — and the reason we embarked upon this book in the first place. Are our great universities ready to assume the responsibility that has been placed upon them? Our answer is that they have no choice and must rise to the challenge at this moment in history.[12] To do otherwise is to cede to the private sector and government a role for which universities are particularly well suited and upon which their long-term viability depends. In many ways, universities are ready to take on the daunting challenge before them, but there is, we feel, a missing ingredient: entrepreneurial thinking. The impact of innovation increases when entrepreneurs are involved. They supply the spark, the passion, and the commitment that inspire creative people to come together and achieve extraordinary things.

High-impact innovation requires an entrepreneurial mindset that views big problems as big opportunities. The entrepreneur is ready to embark on a journey without knowing the exact destination and is ready to fail in reaching for success. When entrepreneurs and entrepreneurial thinking are injected into the mix, remarkable things happen at our great universities. Many universities were founded as a result of a partnership between an academic, often a humanist, and an entrepreneur. Throughout the book, we point to great achievements growing out of an entrepreneurial mindset or from the deep involvement of entrepreneurs in the university community; but these achievements are still too rare, and academics still too often equate entrepreneurship with opportunism or commercialization in a pejorative way.

So let us be clear. We see entrepreneurship as fully consonant with the aims of the modern university, in all its many and varied parts. "Entrepreneurs innovate." These two words by Peter Drucker summarize both his thinking on the meaning of entrepreneurship and literally hundreds of books on the subject.[13] The elegance of the definition makes it easy to miss its profound implications. Notice there is no mention of business. Entrepreneurs are not necessarily business people. Nor do the words "management" or "commercialization" or "finance" or even "money" appear in the definition. Instead, Drucker's definition provides a metaphorical big tent—an intellectual framework—with room for social, scientific, artistic, and, yes, even academic entrepreneurs. This "big tent" actually hosts a conversation, a way of thinking about opportunity, using a set of tools that are available to all no matter what their agenda or their values. Once these ground rules are established, we believe it is appropriate and even imperative that entrepreneurship enter the dialogue that takes place at America's great research universities. The result will be the kind of innovation that will reenergize all of our great institutions in the twenty-first century, as it has in the past.

The word "entrepreneur" was coined around 1800 by the French economist J. B. Say, and it literally means "to take action." More specifically, Say defined the entrepreneur as one who "shifts . . . resources out of an area of lower and into an area of higher productivity."[14] Although the word "entrepreneur" was coined by an economist and formed the basis for an important economic theory, modern thinkers have concluded that the economic approaches described by Say can be applied to virtually all spheres of society. An entrepreneur can just as easily practice in the artistic or social realm as the commercial using the same basic mindset and tools. Wherever he or she operates, however, it is safe to say that the entrepreneur will be functioning as a "change agent," and this notion is at the core of the modern-day definition of "entrepreneur."

There is more than one entrepreneurial personality, and our experience is that all kinds of people can be taught to think like an entrepreneur. Entrepreneurs do, however, share a set of common attributes. They are willing to live with risk and uncertainty because the world they inhabit is highly unpredictable. They are not afraid to fail. They are willing to venture outside their comfort zone and to be what those in the liberal arts call "life-long learners." Because so much of what entrepreneurs do has not yet been invented, they are willing to make it up as they go along. Most important, entrepreneurs are comfortable with ambiguity. The fact that there is no right answer is reassuring to them, perhaps because they were never the smartest kid in the class.

Just as we have attempted to broaden the conventional definition of entrepreneur, we believe the popular understanding of the word "innovation" captures only a small part of its meaning. Curing cancer, sending a rocket to the moon, or inventing the microchip is what most likely comes to mind in response to the word. But the reality is much more complex and nuanced. Rather than a big idea that is going to change the world overnight, innovation is more likely a subtle twist in approaching a problem. Innovation almost always involves change, but as often as not it is the change of a process or way of doing things as opposed to the invention of a better mouse trap. Not surprisingly, innovation is almost always driven by *somebody* (typically an entrepreneur), not an institution or a listserv or a committee.

Entrepreneurship, then, is not a subject or a discipline, but a practice or a way of thinking that can increase the impact of innovation. As we have indicated, it is not characterized solely by an "a-ha moment," but rather a series of actions and decisions that translate a good idea into reality. The revolutionary idea is important for innovation, but it is not sufficient. Even less-than-stellar ideas, as veteran entrepreneurs know, can be turned into outstanding enterprises through a process of synthesis, refinement, and relentless execution.

So to succeed in a university setting, entrepreneurship must be clearly defined as a necessary ingredient for innovation, a particular approach to solving problems, and a complement to—not a substitute for—the critical methods that are fundamental to the liberal arts and sciences. It must not be viewed as mere commercialization, wealth accumulation, or management. The fundamental entrepreneurial mindset, and the techniques that go with it, are the same no matter what your interests, dreams, and values happen to be. This principle is the abiding counterpart to our conviction that ours is the era of entrepreneurship. Global forces have converged to enable individuals and small groups to undertake projects and enterprises of the kind that were once reserved only for large institutions. Large institutions are called upon to incorporate that same approach and way of thinking as a means of dramatically increasing the impact and efficiency of all that they do.

Entrepreneurs balance the need to articulate a broad strategic vision with the need to execute the day-to-day activities that translate the vision into reality. The two distinct sections of this book reflect this dynamic. The first half of the book (Chapters 1–5) is about innovation. It paints a broad vision of the various components of an entrepreneurial university, with the understanding that these chapters are aspirational in nature. Using examples from our own campus and others, we discuss an entrepreneurial approach to science, a variety of social entrepreneurship projects, mechanisms for enterprise creation, and a problem-based, multidisciplinary approach to the world's biggest problems that includes the arts, the sciences, and the professions. The second half of the book (Chapters 6–11) focuses upon skillful and thoughtful execution. We discuss specific approaches required to achieve our vision, such as the collaboration of academic leaders, faculty, and alumni. We also describe an organizational structure and an approach to measuring success—both of which are critical to implementation. This nuts-and-bolts approach is a critical and often-overlooked requirement for success.

We hope our ideas for the future of the university will provoke an important conversation on campuses across the nation and among stakeholders in the future of these institutions. The opportunities facing American research universities have never been more significant, and the stakes have never been higher. In these times, few things could be more exciting than unlocking the promise of one of America's greatest institutions, and we hope this book will, in some way, contribute to that process.

1

The Entrepreneurial Opportunity

Events have conspired to place our great universities in an either enviable or terrifying position, depending on your point of view. They are collectively among the most affluent institutions in our society.[1] They are populated with the best minds in the world and have created a culture that encourages new knowledge and puts it to practical use. But such a wealth of resources comes with an imposing responsibility. Donors, grant makers, and the public at large expect big things from what can reasonably be characterized as one of the crown jewels of our society. Having accumulated such significant resources in the name of advancing society, universities have no choice but to embrace the challenge, but those of us inside the academy know it will be no easy task to meet the high expectations we have created. We believe this moment in history makes unlocking the innovative potential of our research universities a national imperative, and an entrepreneurial mindset is key to achieving this objective.

Five historical trends support our conclusion. First, the problems of the twenty-first century are big and complex. Attacking them will require unprecedented resources and nontraditional approaches that complement traditional academic disciplines. Second, information-based tools at the disposal of individuals and small groups undermine the authority of large bureaucratic institutions and empower those with an entrepreneurial mindset. Third, the students who are the heart and soul of all great universities approach their education and the world with a new and different mindset—one that values results over process and is comfortable with the accumulation of knowledge through complex forms of social networking. Fourth, traditional sources of expendable funds are decreasing, and funders of all forms have performance-based expectations that are best addressed by an entrepreneurial approach. Finally, it has become increasingly obvious that new ways of problem solving that combine traditional rationality with creative solutions will be required to address the world's great problems. Entrepreneurial thinking is central to this new approach.

Big Problems Require a New Approach to Innovation

A research university attacking a small problem is like a brain surgeon performing an appendectomy. With unprecedented resources available to our great American universities and an academic culture built for discovering novel approaches, the public has thrust upon these institutions the challenge of solving what professor John Kao, in his book *Innovation Nation*, calls "wicked problems": climate change, environmental degradation, communicable diseases, and extreme poverty, among others; and a meaningful response is expected.[2] Wicked problems, in Kao's view, have a good deal in common: they rarely have clear-cut solutions that can be unlocked by a single discipline; they are complex and ambiguous; and they require fundamentally new approaches to the status quo.

Wicked problems are fundamentally different from big challenges the United States has tackled in the recent past. For example, the Manhattan Project was created in 1941 to address the belief that Nazi Germany was on the brink of building an atomic bomb that that would lead to an Allied defeat in World War II. Founded upon a series of breakthroughs in theoretical physics, the effort employed 125,000 people at its peak in three key sites under the leadership of one great scientist, Robert Oppenheimer. This vast project had clearly defined goals: to meet an impossible deadline, produce the first nuclear weapon, and ultimately result in an Allied victory. They were achieved with the detonation of two bombs at Hiroshima and Nagasaki and the subsequent surrender of the Japanese forces. All of this was accomplished in three years after the project was authorized by the highest levels of the U.S. government and was successfully kept secret.

The mission to "put a man on the moon" has a similar history. In this case the impetus to innovate came in 1957 from the Russians' launching of an unmanned satellite, Sputnik. Coming at the height of the Cold War, Sputnik's ascent ignited a furor in the United States over the perceived diminution of American scientific and military leadership. With the help of a group of German scientists led by Wernher von Braun, the United States matched the Russian feat of orbit within a year. The National Aeronautics and Space Administration (NASA) was founded soon after with the goal of achieving American preeminence in space travel and eventually placing a man on the moon. Three years later, NASA achieved a fifteen-minute suborbital flight piloted by Alan Shepard, and less than a year later John Glenn orbited the earth. Project Apollo and the race to the moon had begun in earnest, and after a series of difficulties and tragedies, including the death of three astronauts in a training exercise in June of 1969, Apollo 11 landed the first man on the moon. NASA, like the Manhattan Project, achieved rapid success by sticking to a proven approach: combine a strong leader with a clear mission, high-level government commitment, and massive amounts of government funds.

As difficult as it was to build an atomic bomb in three years or to put a man on the moon in twelve, it is tempting to wish that today's wicked problems were more like those earlier challenges, with a clear beginning and end—and a mission that can be clearly stated in a few words. Compare those earlier missions with what must be done to attack twenty-first-century challenges. Their complexity requires cooperation from a variety of disciplines. In fact, these problems are of such magnitude that no single institution can adequately take them on. These problems cross national borders and require international consensus. Their international nature makes funding complex; unlike the Manhattan Project or the NASA mission, no single government or source of funds can achieve success. Most important, these problems are not ones merely of theory or scientific innovation; in fact they are largely impervious to traditional academic problem solving. Addressing complex problems requires diverse points of view, a deep level of practical implementation, and openness to fundamental change. At bottom, they require, in the words of Professor Kao, "integrative approaches that blend necessary perspectives into a new way of doing the actual work of innovation."[3]

The challenge posed by climate change illustrates the need for this new, more entrepreneurial approach. Rising gas prices have accomplished what Al Gore's movie and thousands of scientific articles failed to do in terms of public education, and the world is now aware that its approach to consuming energy must change and a vast array of disciplines must participate in mapping a sustainable course of action. New knowledge is needed in many areas: fuel-cell technology, biofuels, and heat absorption, to name a few. Process improvements in construction and waste removal are essential. Architectural innovations that make green buildings practical and breakthroughs in city planning that reduce or eliminate the need for cars will need to correspond with research in economics, public policy, psychology, sociology, anthropology, and political science. Coordination of these diverse disciplines, and the diverse funding sources that accompany them, will be needed to address the problem, and all these efforts must ultimately have global applicability. Ultimately, solutions must be validated by market forces and consumer behavior.

As tough as they are to solve, our current problems can be viewed as opportunities. To address them, universities must break out of the traditional, hierarchical model that worked so well for the Manhattan Project and the manned space initiative and actually change the way they approach the process of innovation. Accepting the challenges posed by wicked problems will force universities to rethink the way they approach many of their most basic functions.

New Tools Are Empowering Individuals

The complexity of wicked problems is partially offset by the remarkable information-based tools available to virtually anyone on the planet with a computer (or a mobile telecommunications device) and high-speed Internet access. In the United States, some estimate that two-thirds of the population has Internet access and 50 percent has a high-speed line.[4] Sixteen million South Koreans, one out of three, have web pages, and it is estimated that approximately half the world has cell phone access.[5] With a dramatic drop projected in the cost of computers and mobile devices and the expectation that up to 90 percent of the world's population will soon have access to high-speed telecommunications, universal connectivity is no longer a pipe dream.

At the same time that information appliances are proliferating at an astounding rate, the world's knowledge is being digitized, making it accessible to anyone with a cell phone or a laptop computer. Google is spending billions on efforts to put the world's great libraries online, and hundreds of other efforts are aiming to include not only text but audio and video in the new electronic canon—and all of this will be updated in real time. At the most basic level, access to the world's knowledge is being democratized. Although the economics have yet to be worked out (fertile ground for entrepreneurial thinking), what only a few years ago seemed to be a futurist's musings is now happening, and anyone who doubts the new reality should have a look at Google Scholar, the forerunner of the promise of universal knowledge access.

This kind of access is inherently empowering and democratizing. Physical and economic barriers to the free flow of knowledge are going away. What will that mean? A look outside academia provides some hints. A home buyer about to "lock in" a financing option has access to information on the direction of interest rates, including detailed charts, analysis, and predictions previously available only to bankers and traders. A farmer in a small village in India has cell phone access to global crop prices as well as short- and long-term weather reports that make his land more productive and profitable. That same farmer can use a cell phone to determine whether the local health clinic will be open the next day and save a lost day of work if the doctor is not available. The list goes on and on and the message is clear: information that was formerly available only to large institutions is now in the hands of virtually everyone, giving individuals and small groups the power and influence previously reserved for the very few. It is much too early to assess the impact of this "knowledge proliferation," but it has the potential to engage the individual innovator and a band of followers in dialogue that was previously closed to them. Since entrepreneurship almost always starts with an individual and not some committee or institution, the promise of universal access to knowledge creates unprecedented opportunity for anyone with a better idea. If knowledge is the energy that runs the academy's innovation engine, that energy is now essentially free and available to all, 24/7.

The Internet is creating an even more fundamental change in the way knowledge is created, and it points to a central role for entrepreneurship as a catalyst for university-based innovation. All of the examples given so far involve top-down information flows. Those seeking information turn to scholarly experts, professionally prepared databases, or reported market information in order to make decisions or draw conclusions. This is the traditional student-teacher approach that Plato and Socrates canonized and that has remained essentially unchanged ever since—that is, until now. In the last five years, as so much of the world has become digitally literate, information flows have become multidirectional. Wikipedia is the quintessential example: with 1.8 million entries (as compared to 120,000 in the *Encyclopedia Britannica*) and growing at a rate of 1,500 entries a day in English alone, it is by far the world's largest encyclopedia. And entries are constantly updated. When leading television news commentator Tim Russert died unexpectedly of a heart attack, the first public notice of his death (even before it was announced by NBC — his own network) appeared in an update of his Wikipedia entry. Collaborative websites known as wikis are now everywhere, demonstrating the ethic of collaboration John Kao suggests in describing "systems without a center that nevertheless exhibit forceful and creative behaviors." Kao calls these virtual entities the "digital nervous systems of innovation."[6]

The power of these systems is only now beginning to be understood. In retrospect, the U.S. presidential campaign of 2008 may be seen as the coming-out party of the digital nervous system. The most important news scoops of the primaries came not from established newspapers or cable news but from networks of part-time bloggers — many of whom followed the candidates on their own nickel. One, Mayhew Fowler, revealed disparaging remarks Senator Obama made about Pennsylvania voters. Websites such as the Huffington Post, which is essentially an amalgam of blogs, became a cited source for mainstream media outlets as the process of gathering political news was turned on its head. The placement of homemade video clips of candidate appearances on the popular website YouTube confronted candidates with the prospect that their every word might be made available to a worldwide audience.

At the same time, the process of financing political campaigns was being revolutionized. Political action committees such as ActBlue, a conduit for the Democratic Party that has raised nearly $100 million from 420,000 donors, are buoyed by small-dollar donations.[7] In his campaign for the Republican nomination, Ron Paul raised nearly $4 million online in a single day.[8] Obama supporters were routinely reminded through social networking sites to participate in campaign events and to make additional donations. In February of 2008 alone, the Obama campaign raised $45 million online — from large and small donors alike. Over the course of the campaign, Obama's online operation raised more than $500 million from 3 million donors; the average donation was $80; of the 6.5 million donations given, 6 million were of $100 or less.[9] Now the Obama administration has put in place the same multidirectional informational tools as a means of improving the efficiency and transparency of government. Groups in opposition to the current administration, such as the Tea Party movement, employ similar techniques. New bills, directives, and initiatives appear routinely on the president's website for study and comment. Always on, multidirectional communication has permeated our political discourse, and it promises to result in dramatic change to the way we govern ourselves.

It is too early to predict the full impact of these vast new flows of multidirectional information. It is clear that new and powerful collaborative tools will emerge to aid those seeking to attack the world's great problems. Individuals and small groups in the field can beta test approaches pioneered in the lab with the results reported in real time. Continuous feedback loops can be built into virtually every experiment or initiative. Full-motion video will become an important communication tool. Complex webs of relationships will take the place of hierarchical one-way information flows—and there is even a new word for the phenomenon, "crowdsourcing." Entrepreneurial thinking will be required to make sense of it all.

Millennial Students Are Transforming the Academy

Great teachers often say that they learn more from their students than their students learn from them, and the current crop of students are emerging as advocates for innovative approaches to modern problems. The demographic diversity of what has come to be known as the "millennial generation," as well as their standards of intellectual achievement, technological facility, social commitment, and entrepreneurial outlook, make them ideal partners in attacking great problems in a practical and timely manner. Their strong idealism combines with an increasing interest in what has come to be known as social entrepreneurship to create an important and influential constituency ready to engage the world's most challenging and exciting issues.

So who are these millennial students? They were born between 1981 and 1993, and they are the largest demographic cohort since the 75 million Baby Boomers. Approximately 40 percent of millennials in America are nonwhite, and 20 percent have a parent who is an immigrant. Eighty percent have participated in some form of community service, and they are generally optimistic about the future. Almost half have an interest in starting their own business, and they generally think of themselves as entrepreneurial.[10] Most significantly, they have integrated into their lives technology that even the most imaginative futurist could not have anticipated a decade ago. A 2007 study found that 97 percent of millennials own a computer and 94 percent own a cell phone; 76 percent use instant messaging to stay connected 24/7. A third of millennials use the Web as their primary source of news, and an equal number author a blog. Half of them download their music using peer-to-peer file-sharing applications, and 60 percent own a portable music player such as an iPod. Seventy-five percent of those in college have a Facebook account.[11]

This new generation profoundly impacts the classroom and the campus. Classroom discussions are more incisive when laptops are present as fact-checking and information-gathering tools. The phrase "go home and look it up" has been replaced with "someone look it up now." And "looking it up" is no longer confined to print media, with YouTube screening 3 billion videos a month on its site. With social networking sites such as Facebook and Twitter, all members of the campus community have access not only to traditional facts but late-breaking news, local events, unsubstantiated rumors, and more. Being up to date takes on a whole new meaning. Constant communication has an even more profound impact on the campus milieu. Students' time horizons are shorter when messages, music, photos, and information are all instantaneous. What used to take weeks or days now gets done in seconds, and this new reality permeates every aspect of millennials' lives. They expect to get things done quickly and are fully capable of assembling complex teams and significant human and even financial resources to solve problems that are important to them. The tools millennials have at their disposal make them willing to attack tough problems. Jeffrey Sachs's Millennium Project aims at eliminating extreme poverty by the year 2015 and has been embraced and driven by college students throughout the country. Wendy Kopp's vision to give every child a good education has made Teach for America a mainstay employer among the nation's most prestigious universities. Millennials are undaunted when solutions to great challenges are not obvious; their mindset, driven by unprecedented access to information and to one another, makes them willing to tackle enormous problems with optimism and resolve.

The new, millennial student will be more than a willing participant as research universities respond to the problems of our time. More likely they will be drivers of change, challenging the academy to do more and questioning the efficacy of old, hierarchical approaches. They are bright, impatient, idealistic, well armed with technology, and committed to taking on daunting problems. They are yet another force pushing the university toward innovative approaches to big challenges.

Funding Sources Have Higher Expectations

The expectations of those who fund research universities are chang-ing dramatically, and it will take entrepreneurial thinking to respond. For the foreseeable future, it appears that government funding for sci-entific research will decrease, forcing institutions to rely more on pri-vate donors; these donors expect results from their largesse, and they want universities to tackle big problems. Short-term increases in gov-ernment funding will aim at stimulating the economy, and that will mandate innovative approaches that have immediate application to big, real-world problems.

At a macro level, federal funding for research and development as a percentage of gross domestic product in the year 2000 declined to a fifty-year low, and by 2004 it was back to 1954 standards.[12] The 2007 number showed a continuing decrease, and notwithstanding a tem-porary windfall from the stimulus package, it is unlikely that the trend will reverse itself in the near future.[13] For state-supported research universities, the situation is even more difficult. Even before the finan-cial meltdown, state funding for higher education was at a twenty-five-year low, and huge shortfalls have made the situation even more dire. State governments can no longer go it alone in funding their flagship institutions of higher learning. There is an "arms race" for increas-ingly large endowments that requires multibillion-dollar fundraising campaigns. In fact, eighteen of the thirty-three American universities currently seeking to raise at least $1 billion in endowments are state schools, and the most affluent of these schools have all completed campaigns in excess of $2 billion.[14] From a funding point of view, it has become hard to tell the difference between public and private in-stitutions, with both groups looking to nongovernmental sources for their future growth.

The current funding system demands accountability from research universities and an increased emphasis on results. It takes only a few conversations on virtually any university campus to prove the point. Development officers attest that prospective donors have clear ideas about the activities they want to support, and in some cases, they be-come actively engaged in implementing the programs they endow. It is not unusual, for instance, for the benefactors of large, merit-based scholarships to become deeply involved in the selection of recipients and the structuring of the program. Donors to institutes and centers routinely sit on their boards and increasingly demand that clear, mea-surable goals for success be established and met. Gift agreements are now often carefully crafted documents that look more like commercial contracts than acts of philanthropy. In short, private donors are increasingly interested in what gets done with the funds they contribute.

University scientists tell a similar story: money for basic research is harder to come by. Governmental and nongovernmental sources have clear ideas about the research they want to fund, the way that research is conducted, and the results that are required in order to receive further support. Even the most traditional government institutions are now adopting an "output-oriented" strategy, for which impact is an important criteria. Agencies traditionally at the forefront of the sponsorship of basic research, such as the National Science Foundation and the National Institutes of Health, are making grants under new programs that require the projects to show potential for commercialization and public benefit.

This move toward accountability is impacting not only new money but also traditional operating funds. At the University of Minnesota, the general administration has asked each of the system's thirty-two state universities to prepare a "dashboard" updated on a regular basis that reports on performance against well-defined metrics. At bottom, accountability is about successful execution—analyzing outputs as compared to initial expectations, making midcourse corrections and, ultimately, hard decisions, since not all programs and initiatives will succeed. Increased accountability within the academy will require just this kind of mindset—a passion for attacking large problems, a willingness to measure how the effort is going, a commitment to midcourse corrections based upon facts, and an understanding that success is not guaranteed and that failure is a possibility.

Big Problems Require New Approaches to Problem Solving

Big, complex problems have a way of humbling the greatest minds. Consider prostate cancer. Decades of research and billions of dollars have led to the understanding that neither doctors, chemists, biologists, nor engineers can arrive at a cure on their own. When an answer does emerge, it will be the work of multidisciplinary teams with members from traditional and perhaps nontraditional areas of knowledge. And team members will not only come from different disciplines, but they will employ different ways of thinking. In his book *Five Minds for the Future*, Professor Howard Gardner of Harvard University explains that traditional problems can often be solved with one mind, and in academia this is what Gardner describes as the "disciplined mind." You might think of this person as a knowledge worker, the smartest kid in the class, the best information processor, who can read, retain, and recall data better than any of her peers. But solving the complex problems of today requires Gardner's four other minds as well. The "synthesizing mind" is necessary to understand how to apply insights learned in a test tube to experiments with mice and eventually human subjects. The "creating mind" is required to go to the next level and develop entirely new approaches when the synthesis of traditional disciplines fails. All of this requires a high degree of cooperation (the "respectful mind") and a careful adherence to moral principles (the "ethical mind").

This multifaceted approach is gaining acceptance among the various stakeholders concerned with solving great problems. Foundations and government funding sources often require investigators from multiple disciplines, as well as measurable and, in some cases, commercially applicable results as a condition of funding. The Department of Defense has launched a Synergistic Idea Development Award to encourage researchers from different disciplines to undertake high-risk/high-gain approaches to address a central problem or question. The Prostate Cancer Foundation (PCF) has funded a similar approach, PCF Challenge Awards, aimed at teams of at least three highly experienced investigators from one or several institutions focusing on high-impact solutions that manifest originality, innovation, and attention toward clinical translation and ultimate patient benefit. Accordingly, academics are organizing themselves—at least partly in response to funding opportunities—into multidisciplinary groups.

Notwithstanding its attractiveness, a multifaceted approach will, more often than not, fail without entrepreneurial thinking—that is, seeing the big picture or integrating and imagining how the pieces fit together. We would hasten to add that in the world of complex problems, seeing the big picture is required but not enough. To be successful, the entrepreneurial thinker must also be accomplished in one or more disciplines, a good team player (or more likely a team builder), and highly ethical because of the profound societal issues that are often involved.

Entrepreneurship Is the Missing Ingredient

Since time immemorial, humankind has been drawn to special places where, it is believed, one can tap into the mysterious unknown. Human beings have long believed that certain places—the Grand Canyon, Mont Blanc, Devil's Tower in Wyoming, the Ganges River—hold a mysterious power to enlighten the mind, inspire creativity, and awaken the soul to its true purpose. In many of these places, people have erected temples or other ritual structures: think of Delphi, Machu Picchu, Stonehenge, and the Pyramids. What makes these places special—in addition to their inherent qualities—is the fact that when we go there, we open ourselves to absorb what we don't know. We free ourselves of our preconceptions. Instead of talking, we allow the "wit and wisdom of the place," as an old Chinese saying puts it, to speak to us.[15]

You might guess this is a description of the modern research university by Alfred North Whitehead, Derek Bok, Bart Giamatti, or Frank Rhodes, all preeminent academic leaders who have written elegantly on the virtues of American higher education. With slight alteration this description could also fit a classic liberal education exposing students to a variety of disciplines, teaching them to learn, and exploring new ways of doing and thinking. The description actually comes from John Kao's *Innovation Nation* and portrays the kind of environment he believes is required to tackle the world's biggest problems. After years of studying and teaching innovation, Kao has concluded "there is a wisdom of place," and at least from our perspective, that place looks much like a university. Yet next to the word "university" in the index to Kao's book the words "See Education" appear, and in the section of the book on the importance of place to innovation, no mention is made of universities.

How can this be? Don't the smartest people in our society gravitate toward academic communities? Isn't academia known for discovering new ways of doing and seeing things? Didn't the World Wide Web get started to foster knowledge sharing among academics, and wasn't social networking (the newest form of knowledge transfer) invented by undergraduates on a college campus? And in terms of resources, what institutions in our society have more financial resources dedicated to attacking the world's big problems? There is obviously something missing in the mix, and we believe, as you might expect, the missing ingredient is entrepreneurship.

We are not suggesting that entrepreneurship is "the answer" but rather the missing ingredient when almost everything else is in place. If entrepreneurial thinking can be introduced and integrated into the dialogue on the campuses of our great universities, these institutions can emerge as true engines of innovation—just what society expects of them.

2

Entrepreneurial Science

At even the most traditional research universities, the science buildings stand out. They are bigger, newer, and bristling with technology. These modern temples are often designed to blend modestly with older campus architecture only to betray their purpose with complex air-handling systems and satellite dishes crowding the roof. Although the campus tour guide may describe these buildings as chemistry or biology departments, and the directory on the first floor may list a department chair or the location of administrative offices, no simple organizational chart can describe the complex set of relationships that drive and finance a top-flight department in the physical or biological sciences. Traditionally, the heart of all of these enterprises is a laboratory led by a tenured professor, staffed by undergraduate, graduate, and postdoctoral students, and supported with millions of dollars of equipment. After a $1 to $2 million initial investment, a lab's annual operating budget can range between $500,000 and $5 million depending on the lab's size. Nearly all of the ongoing support for these labs comes from public and private sources in the form of general and sponsored research grants. The top twenty research institutions receive more than a third of roughly $30 billion awarded annually in federal research funds, and the top one hundred receive close to 80 percent. Supported by a total pool of nearly $50 billion, science has become central to the economic model of every research university.[1]

One list of the world's biggest problems would include climate change, communicable diseases, extreme poverty, overreliance on nonrenewable energy sources, environmental degradation, poor water quality, and nuclear proliferation. Science plays a central role in addressing all of these issues. A look at the funding patterns of some of the world's largest private foundations and donors illustrates the point. The Bill and Melinda Gates Foundation's Grand Challenges in Global Health committed $450 million to help scientists find solutions to revolutionize prevention and treatment of disease in developing countries.[2] The priorities the Gates Foundation has established for its global health care program—acute diarrheal illness, acute lower respiratory infections, child health, HIV/AIDS, malaria, nutrition, reproductive health, vaccines, tuberculosis, and other infectious diseases—all involve intensive scientific research. Other leading funding sources, both public and private, have followed suit with targeted, results-oriented grants programs. The Milken Prostate Cancer Foundation has provided $350 million to more than 1,500 scientific research projects; the Sandler Supporting Foundation (recently the recipient of a $1.3 billion bequest) has focused on asthma and malaria research and devoted more than $100 million to university centers dedicated to applied scientific research.[3]

These bequests are not only large, they are hugely influential. When Bill and Melinda Gates and their partner Warren Buffett speak, people listen. The Gateses' heavy bet on the natural sciences had a profound influence on private foundations and governments. The bottom line: even in difficult financial times large amounts of funding for the sciences will be available to attack big problems, and research universities are the logical place for much of that funding to go. To attract and maximize the impact of such funding, universities must embrace what we call entrepreneurial science: a high-impact, problem-based approach to the world's biggest problems that produces measurable results in terms of public benefit.

First some background. Not surprisingly, the increasing importance of scientific research to the university's economic model has generated heated discussion outside and inside academia. An influential senator looks at the vast sums of federal money being allocated to research labs and questions the return on that investment. A thoughtful critic wonders why our great universities are not having a more profound impact on the world's biggest problems. A state lawmaker criticizes public universities for failing to produce more economic development in the form of small businesses and new jobs. An entrepreneurial alumnus criticizes the slow pace of the technology transfer process whereby new ideas are turned over to commercial enterprise through licensing deals or the creation of spin-out companies.

Inside the university, some academics worry that the emphasis on applied science required by outside funding sources negatively impacts the practice of basic or "pure" science. They cite the demise or dramatic reduction of private funds for research labs such as the Palo Alto Research Center (PARC) in California and Bell Labs on the East Coast as evidence that the research university has become the last refuge for pure scientific research that leads to huge breakthroughs, spawns new products and industries, and impacts the world's biggest problems. They also argue that the 1980 Bayh-Dole Act, federal legislation designed to increase the number of university patents, as well as cooperation between academia and the private sector, has had a series of unintended consequences including a dramatic constriction in the openness of academic research, the subordination of the interests of the scientist to the interests of the institution, and an increase in the influence of corporations and government on the kind of work that goes on in the university.

Some of this criticism is valid, but much of it harkens back to an earlier era. The days when a single scientist worked alone or with a small group over many years to produce a body of work worthy of a Nobel Prize are mostly past. Of course, the old model still works occasionally. At our own university, Oliver Smithies was awarded the 2007 Nobel Prize in medicine after a lifetime of exhaustive research. It is clear, however, that funding for basic research will be increasingly difficult to obtain, and, in the future, problem-based or applied research will be the rule and not the exception.

The Langer Lab

What is entrepreneurial science? One of the best examples is the Langer Lab at the Massachusetts Institute of Technology (MIT), and, like virtually every entrepreneurial success story we know of, this one begins not with a committee or a program but with an individual—in this case Bob Langer. Recently referred to as the Thomas Edison of our generation, Dr. Langer is one of the world's most prolific inventors, with over 500 patents to his credit, and the winner of virtually every major science prize. Educated as a chemical engineer, he has launched more than a dozen start-up companies and more than one hundred licensing deals, and the science that underpins these commercial transactions is stunning in its breadth and depth. But what is most exciting about Bob Langer, and the reason we highlight his work here, is the complex information flow that informs his research and enables him to focus on solutions to problems that, in his own words, will "change the world."

Langer began his career as a square peg in a round hole. After receiving an Sc.D. in chemical engineering from MIT in 1979, he was more interested in solving important problems than advancing along a predictable career path. He rejected four job offers from Exxon alone and set out to find a medical school where his background in chemical engineering might serve various disciplines and research approaches. He finally landed a job at a Harvard surgical research lab headed by Dr. Judah Folkman and engaged in studying ways to prevent the formation of blood vessels in tumors. The lab's research showed that large molecules in cartilage prevent the growth of blood vessels, but targeted delivery of large-molecule drugs was science that was new to the world. Langer developed a novel approach to the drug delivery quandary that was universally rejected by many of the world's most renowned scientists, including two Nobel Prize winners.

Undaunted, Langer moved to MIT, where he found a home among an eclectic mix of professors in the Department of Applied Biological Sciences—the chemistry department from which he graduated was not interested in hiring him. In his first year he was turned down for nine research grants, and his prospects were grim. But Langer continued with what can only be characterized as a bold research agenda: he created a culture in his lab that embraced high-risk, high-impact projects.

As his lab grew in both human and financial resources, Langer never wavered from his determination, in the words of a colleague, "to go after problems that can change the world" within a context of "scientific excellence." Another colleague characterizes Langer as "totally an idea guy" but "not threatened by being in an environment where he is not the expert. . . . [He] has a great eye for impact, great instinct. He will take chances that many people wouldn't take." One colleague believes Langer's greatest accomplishment is the creation of the 120 professors (graduates of his lab) who are trying to follow in his footsteps at other institutions. Perhaps Langer sums up his own success best: "So many times when you try to do something in science, when you try to invent something, people tell you that it's impossible, that it will never work. But I think that is very rarely true. I think if you really believe in yourself, if you really stick to things, there is very little that is really impossible."[4]

The Langer Lab is the largest biomedical engineering lab in the world. Based in the Whitaker Health Sciences building at MIT, it takes up most of the third floor and involves approximately one hundred researchers and an annual budget in excess of $10,000,000. Each year roughly 6,000 graduate students and postdocs apply for five open positions. Working at the intersection between biotechnology and materials science, the lab studies and develops polymers that deliver drugs at controlled rates for prolonged periods of time. This work has spawned myriad products and companies including a firm that manufactures drug inhalation products, a method for delivering drugs using microprocessors, and a waterproof bandage inspired by the adhesive pads on a gecko's feet.[5] The lab's open architecture reflects a culture that attracts researchers who are focused on problem solving in a multidisciplinary environment. Langer's leadership style empowers highly motivated individuals who are willing to take risks and look at the world differently.[6]

The remarkable group of people who inform Langer and the research of his lab may be the "secret sauce" that has given rise to his remarkable success. In a representational sketch of Langer's professional network for a case about Langer and his lab in the *Harvard Business Review*, a total of twenty-one high-level contacts are illustrated.[7] These contacts include partners at venture capital funds, university administrators, medical practitioners, senior members of the Langer Lab, government officials, executives from private foundations, senior research professors, and executives from high-growth and Fortune 500 companies. The map places Langer at the center of this complex web. By all accounts he is an open-minded listener and generously shares what he learns with others. Langer also values commercial input on practical questions that guide research. As a result of his broadmindedness, Langer is in a position to intuitively evaluate what we have called "impact." With a few phone calls and a series of discussions, Langer's network enables him to quickly assess the scientific, social, and commercial dimensions of a project.

The commercialization model for the Langer Lab is simple, but it works. First, a "huge" idea grows out of work in the lab. According to Langer, this idea will address a societal need through the invention of a platform product. Next, Langer identifies and empowers an entrepreneurial champion. If the idea proves promising and the scientific underpinnings are solid, a "seminal paper" and a blocking patent are prepared with the idea that the patent is to be filed prior to publication of the research. Although seed money to commercialize the work is typically needed at this stage, Langer likes to delay raising significant capital until publication makes it more likely that a patent will be issued. The published paper typically generates a huge amount of media attention and stokes interest from venture capitalists—Langer has a longstanding relationship with one venture capitalist and access to many others if necessary—making possible the capitalization of the project on favorable terms. Depending on the nature of the invention, the final step usually involves in vivo studies demonstrating the efficacy of the research. This development model has spawned over twenty-five companies and more than thirty-five products either currently on the market or in testing. There is no better example anywhere in the world of a classic spin-out strategy in which big ideas are identified and nurtured inside academe and, when ready, handed off one by one to the private sector for commercialization.

The DeSimone Research Group

A giant of a scientist—literally and figuratively—stands at the center of the DeSimone Research Group. Joe DeSimone is an imposing presence at close to six-and-a-half feet tall, and he looms large in his field as well. Like Langer, DeSimone was a prodigy, earning his Ph.D. at twenty-five. Since joining the Chemistry Department at the University of North Carolina at Chapel Hill in 1990, he has published 250 papers, obtained 80 pending and 119 issued patents, and received numerous awards, including the $500,000 Lemelson-MIT Prize for invention. He is a member of the National Academy of Engineering and the American Academy of Arts and Sciences. Since his arrival at UNC, DeSimone has been interested in two things: the development of new platforms whose application could impact large, intractable problems and the commercialization of the applications that are spawned by such platforms. The unique approach DeSimone and UNC have to his two interests suggests a method that is fundamentally different from the one pursued by Langer and MIT.

A native of Norristown, Pennsylvania, and the son of an accountant and a tailor, DeSimone grew up in an entrepreneurial household. He fondly recalls the days when he and his dad sold model airplanes in the local mall. His inquisitive and meticulous parents inspired in him an interest in science, and he gravitated to nearby Ursinus College for a course offered in polymer chemistry. After obtaining a doctorate from Virginia Tech, DeSimone turned down seventeen jobs in industry, interviewing instead at top-tier chemistry departments. As he tells it, he didn't believe chemistry departments were interviewing *him*, but instead that he was in search of the right department to help advance his ideas on the development of new polymers formed with carbon dioxide—big ideas he had been thinking about for many years. Little did DeSimone know that his interviewers were wary of his résumé; among other shortcomings, he had no postdoctoral training, and department chairs were not at all sure his ideas were viable. He recalls the process: "I had no idea how accomplished the interviewers were. They were members of the National Academy of Sciences and I didn't know what the National Academy was. If I had known I might not have even interviewed." He did intrigue one faculty member at the University of North Carolina, Ed Samulski, a materials chemist interested in launching a polymer program. Samulski thought that Joe was "much more confident and secure in what he was doing than a typical junior professor, and had a big and original idea." The more Samulski thought about DeSimone's big idea, the more excited he became, and eventually Samulski was able to convince his colleagues that DeSimone should be hired.

Upon his arrival at UNC in 1990, DeSimone began demonstrating that combining commercially significant fluoropolymers with carbon dioxide allowed for an environmentally friendly method to manufacture the fluoropolymers. A significant impediment to the synthesis of fluoropolymers prior to DeSimone's discovery was their general insolubility in most solvents except chlorofluorocarbons (CFCs) that are environmentally hazardous. By 1992, he had published his first article in the preeminent journal *Science*, and he published a second two years later. By 1996, DuPont had licensed DeSimone's polymerization technology for the production of Teflon in carbon dioxide, and Hangers Cleaners had been created to employ the technology as a "green" dry-cleaning technique. As he and his colleagues continued to explore the use of supercritical CO_2 for the manufacture of what they dubbed "liquid Teflon," a material also called PFPE (perfluoropolyether), they quickly discovered that PFPE enabled the creation of highly precise patterned films and customizable nanoparticles. The platform DeSimone had been working on immediately took on new significance. It gave rise to a technology he called PRINT (Particle Replication in Non-wetting Templates), used to manufacture precisely designed nanoparticles hundreds of times smaller than a red blood cell.

The opportunity, as DeSimone puts it, is to "achieve the uniformity associated with the micro-electronics industry and apply it to areas such as nanomedicine for the production of targeted therapies and the detection of disease."[8] If the science works, it means that nanoparticles infused with a particular drug can enter and deposit their cargo in a targeted group of cells. The technology also has implications for solar cells and morphable robots, among scores of other applications.

With his vision for the platform fully developed, DeSimone established a company called Liquidia, whose mission is to commercialize all of the PRINT applications developed in the DeSimone lab. In practice, this means that Liquidia, in cooperation with its customers, answers questions critical for commercial acceptance. These questions are often time sensitive and driven by business considerations pertaining to "commercial" as opposed to "academic" science. Liquidia is also a manufacturer and creates technology and know-how that permits the production of nanoscale particles and film. Liquidia's business development function also facilitates deep and complex dialogue with companies in the biotechnology and materials science fields. Exchanges between the DeSimone lab and Liquidia are, for the most part, transparent. Findings from time-sensitive research conducted at Liquidia may be refined in the DeSimone lab and sometimes lead to publishable research. Insights from the lab are passed along to Liquidia, and they may affect a critical commercial experiment or trial. Most important, DeSimone is deeply involved in both enterprises. From his point of view his involvement in both spheres makes "[his] science better" because "pure scientists often have no context."[9]

The arrangement in which one company commercializes all of the PRINT applications was carefully devised by DeSimone and his investors to create a new model of cooperation that, if executed properly, would provide a sustainable competitive advantage. This new model grew out of a number of factors. First, DeSimone revels in the details of his lab's work *and* in the business of Liquidia. Simply turning over the commercialization function for PRINT was, in his view, not an option. Second, the manufacturing function at Liquidia is intimately tied to work going on in the DeSimone lab. A close and relatively open relationship between the two is essential if the lab is to get the molds it needs for particle fabrication and testing and Liquidia is to get the insights the lab can offer as to the creation of the equipment and technology forming the basis of its manufacturing capability. Third, the commercialization process of a number of applications allows Liquidia to develop a series of scientific and business competencies and improve them over time. It is thought that the consolidation of developments in Liquidia will ultimately give the company an advantage over a competitor that spawns a new company for each commercial application. Finally, information flows freely between the lab and Liquidia, with some exceptions involving manufacturing technology and restrictions imposed by commercial partners.

Formal and informal mechanisms have been created to facilitate the free flow of information, and there is a conscious effort to rationalize the work of the two entities. Liquidia formally sponsors certain applications-related research in the lab, but other research indirectly improves upon the PRINT platform. Accordingly, the deep involvement of the DeSimone lab with the commercial world is viewed positively by government agencies and other grant sources anxious for academic research to be aimed at important and ultimately commercially viable problems.

As DeSimone is quick to point out, his model of operation has yet to prove itself—unlike Langer's time-tested approach—despite attracting more than $45 million in venture capital and an investment from the Gates Foundation. The unique relationship between DeSimone's lab and Liquidia also poses conflict-of-interest issues for UNC that have to be addressed on an ongoing basis. Many scientists take issue with DeSimone's assertion that a close tie with Liquidia makes his science better, but objections to his methods are rebutted by the steady stream of publications coming from the lab and the ongoing scientific and commercial recognition of its accomplishments.

Although they employ different approaches, the work of the Langer Lab and the DeSimone Research Group suggest some basic principles that structure the way we think about entrepreneurial science.

An Interdisciplinary Approach Is Essential to Solving Big Scientific Problems

Traditional disciplines such as chemistry, biology, physics, and medicine provide an excellent means of organizing science. This organization is not particularly useful, however, in attacking big problems. When faced with the task of building the first atomic bomb, the U.S. government did not look to a chemistry or physics department or even to the Institute of Advanced Studies at Princeton where Albert Einstein plied his trade. Instead, the Manhattan Project was organized under the direction of Robert Oppenheimer, a theoretical physicist who had never directed an organization, and General Leslie Groves, an engineer whose previous claim to fame was overseeing the construction of the Pentagon. In less than four years the project grew to 125,000 employees. Similarly, Project Apollo, NASA's effort to put a man on the moon, also relied on an interdisciplinary approach. A partnership between a rocket scientist, Wernher von Braun, and master politician Jim Webb was formed in response to Russia's launching of Sputnik in 1957. Twelve years and $135 billion later, NASA put a man on the moon.

Leading research donors also insist on the practice of interdisciplinary science. The Gates Foundation requires an interdisciplinary approach as part of its Grand Challenges program; the National Institutes of Health and the National Science Foundation increasingly require an interdisciplinary approach of their grant recipients; and large private donations to science almost uniformly demand a results-oriented, cross-disciplinary orientation. A recent $100 million bequest to Princeton University by Gerry Andlinger, no neophyte to philanthropy, having previously given over $25 million to Princeton and other institutions, demonstrates the new approach. Andlinger's grant funds research on sustainable solutions to problems of energy and environment through an interdisciplinary center that combines physics, chemistry, and nanotechnology studies to produce innovative materials ready for commercial application. Andlinger is clear about the purpose of the bequest: "Princeton . . . already has substantial work underway on a variety of energy-related and environmental problems. . . . My hope in establishing this center is to bring those strengths together and focus them on finding 'cleantech' solutions to the most important problems facing our society today."[10]

This new approach to university science suggested by those who fund it is necessarily multidisciplinary. Real-world problems cross virtually all traditional disciplinary boundaries, and the people charged with solving those problems should not be constrained by traditional mechanisms for ordering knowledge. Breaking down the academic silos within the university is, however, only the first step toward creating the complex dialogue that supports an entrepreneurial lab and, ultimately, entrepreneurial science.

While we strongly believe that attacking big problems will almost always require a multidisciplinary approach and that universities should encourage interdisciplinary science, we do not advocate the dismantling of the traditional disciplines such as chemistry, physics, and biology. Creating new interdisciplinary units simply increases administrative complexity and additional silos in an organization that already has too many. Encouraging a culture that accepts and promotes interdisciplinary work within the traditional disciplines and across traditional barriers will have a greater impact.

Academic Institutions Should Encourage Academic Science

We recently asked an accomplished scientist charged with running the day-to-day operations of a large academic chemistry lab to list her top two priorities. "Teaching and helping our students get a job," she replied—a great reminder that despite the importance of the research and its potential impact, students remain at the core of the university.[11] In science, the nexus between research and teaching is clear and always on view. Students develop their own careers while doing valuable work in the lab. Whether the student researcher's objective is a doctorate or a publishable paper, his or her aim is to generate "new knowledge," a goal at the heart of academic science. The work must also meet the exacting standards of university research—standards that are often higher in academia than in the private sector. After several years of this low-paying yet highly demanding research, the student can chose from career paths that lead either to continued work in academia as a professor and researcher, toward the private sector and a commercial lab, or occasionally into an independent venture.

If traditional academic science and important basic research are not supported at research universities, other organizations are unlikely to pick up the slack. Moreover, no other institution provides the human and financial capital—or the intellectual freedom—to pursue new knowledge outside the constraints imposed by the marketplace or government. In addition, the culture developed in academic institutions and the communities that surround them attracts individuals who are prepared to trade a high salary for the freedom to pursue their interests. The disciplines themselves also provide a set of role models, a built-in "jury" in the form of dissertation committees and journal editors and a long and illustrious history all designed to encourage great scientists and great science. It's easy to dismiss the value of academic science in a rush to solve the world's biggest problems. We think that is a false choice and that the world is looking to academia to provide innovative approaches to serious problems precisely because of the value it ascribes to academic science.

External Funding Can Make Academic Science Better

Research in the DeSimone lab at UNC involves direct costs of approximately $3 million over six years. Some in the academy worry that the panoply of funding sources required to fund a lab can result in scientific decisions being dictated by external sources whose motives are inconsistent with the values of the university. DeSimone, as we already noted, sees this differently: he feels that the work he does with Liquidia and the contact with other companies makes his science better. DeSimone believes that scientists are poor judges of the impact of their research and that the private sector can offer academic science the kind of feedback that can come only through interaction with customers and the marketplace. Collaboration can also provide academics with a "quick look" at a possible solution from the private sector that can then be incorporated into more formal scientific research. Similarly, "skunkworks," or small groups of researchers that focus on a particular issue, often make discoveries in academic laboratories with immediate commercial applications. Government and private grants also encourage the dissemination of information through conferences and other forms of collaboration and encourage a free flow of information among like-minded researchers—a development that can lead to better science. When the process of collaboration works correctly, there is a free flow of information that makes both academic and commercial science better. But external funding does more than facilitate information sharing. Grantors and sponsors are increasingly likely to require measurable goals and specific time frames for results that provide needed focus to academic research. Labs guided by an external donor house a culture that focuses on outputs and results and therefore increases the impact of the work that is being supported.

Geography Cannot Drive the Train

Funding and commercializing science is extraordinarily difficult. Encouraging science to have the impact we have described makes sense, but defining the geographical location of that impact does not. Science needs to gravitate to the location where it is mostly likely to succeed. In many cases that means it stays close to the place where it was conceived because a natural parent, all other things being equal, is superior to a foster parent. To the extent the inventor or the founding lab can stay connected to the science as it develops the science benefits. The kind of communication and complex relationships we advocate ideally take place when the parties involved work in the same building, on the same campus, or in the same neighborhood. All of the examples of collaboration we detail in this chapter involve geographic proximity, and proximity is to be encouraged. But there are instances when other considerations take precedence. In some cases, private funding sources want spin-out companies close by in order to provide the hands-on supervision new ventures require. In other cases, folding an invention into an existing lab dramatically increases the likelihood of success. In such cases, it may be necessary for research to relocate. Such a move may mean that jobs are created and economic development takes place far from where the invention was conceived. In our view, such dislocations have a way of evening out. If a research university creates a great environment for science inside and outside its walls, it will generate its fair share of economic development, but the insistence that science be commercialized where it is conceived is unrealistic and ultimately unproductive.

Use Technology Transfer as a Tool for Faculty Retention

Since the passage of the Bayh-Dole Act in 1980, every research university has established a technology transfer office designed to commercialize the inventions developed at the university and generate licensing and royalty income—and in some cases capital gains—for the university. Typically these offices are overcommitted, understaffed, and burdened with expectations that they will pay for themselves and earn great sums for their university. Tech transfer offices rarely fulfill such lofty expectations. With a very few exceptions, universities have not gotten rich on technology transfer. The advent of the Bayh-Dole Act has spawned a $43 billion-a-year biotech industry, and intellectual property rights have historically netted universities over a billion dollars a year, but roughly a third of new discoveries and nearly half of all licensing income goes to only ten schools. The biggest winner was Emtriva, an AIDS drug invented at Emory University that resulted in a royalty payment of $320 million after fees and 40 percent paid to three initial investors; another big winner was the University of Florida with more than $80 million reaped from Gatorade to date. Columbia's patent of Axel's genetic engineering techniques netted $600 million over twenty years. Entrepreneurial science will improve the record of unmet expectations, but we believe commercial success should be only one criterion used to measure scientific impact.

Research universities ought to worry less about the revenue their technology transfer offices produce and more about how those offices can be used as an instrument for faculty recruitment and retention. By making it easier for faculty to obtain patents and negotiate license deals and spin-out companies, the university keeps faculty engaged and connected and therefore less likely to leave. Providing faculty with equity ownership is cheaper than a salary increase, especially if money for an increase must come from an endowment where, typically, only 5 percent per year is expendable. Even if the new invention does not result in a great return—and this is usually the case—the inventor often ascribes great value to the equity interest granted. The university gets credit not only for the sums that flow to the faculty member but also for those that are expected to flow sometime in the future.

There are other reasons to invest in technology transfer and to streamline the commercialization of academic science. Although few in number, companies that spin out of universities are disproportionately high performing; one study estimates that 8 percent of spin-outs go public, over twice the rate of U.S. enterprises generally.[12] Streamlining the commercialization process by deemphasizing concerns about financial returns, and adopting a more uniform, faculty-friendly approach will result in the creation of more companies in a timely manner and increase the likelihood of commercial success. Finally, faculty who achieve success in commercializing their work are well situated to make important financial contributions to the institutions that spawned their success. They should be carefully solicited by those charged with university development.

Faculty retention is an important measure in evaluating the effectiveness of a technology transfer office, and metrics should be established to determine how well the goal is being achieved. An indirect effect of such metrics may be better science and the creation of more spin-outs, a result that would be well received by those concerned about the impact of university research.

Entrepreneurial Science Requires Entrepreneurial Thinking

So how do we reconcile academic science with what we call entrepreneurial science? Most scientists would say there is a clear line between the discovery of new knowledge fundamental to academia's mission and the commercialization of that knowledge, which takes place primarily in the private sector. The distinction between the two endeavors is important; commercialization is hard enough without adding the confining structure of an academic discipline. So where does entrepreneurship fit in? Can academic science also be entrepreneurial science? We think the answer is yes. Entrepreneurial thinking can help answer the threshold question in all of academic research: What new knowledge ought to be pursued? As we have already stated we think the answer revolves around "impact"—the need to discover what new knowledge will have the greatest impact. Entrepreneurial thinking is particularly helpful in seeing the big picture, and in a scientific context this means weaving together all the threads, including the requirements of academic science, an understanding of critical global problems, familiarity of various external funding sources, and a level of comfort with the commercialization process. While entrepreneurial thinking is not the same thing as commercialization, the market does perform a useful function in informing academic science.

Entrepreneurial thinking can be injected into academic science in two ways: scientists can learn to think entrepreneurially, and entrepreneurs can be included in academic endeavors. Peter Drucker contends that systematic innovation can be learned; our own techniques for teaching undergraduates can, we believe, be applied to academics as well. We tested this idea recently at an entrepreneurship "boot camp," where we invited UNC professors to a four-day session designed to equip them with the tools to begin thinking like an entrepreneur. We were encouraged that all of those invited to the session freely chose to attend, and that we had participants from more than ten different disciplines ranging from anthropology to chemistry to medicine.

To the extent that academic science is engaged in a dialogue with the commercial world—as a result of sponsored research or some other similar relationship—entrepreneurial thinking will inform scientific research. Conversely, universities can invite entrepreneurs with relevant experience to join the academic ranks on a full- or part-time basis in order to engage with faculty in making academic science more entrepreneurial. The model for this exchange is the "entrepreneur-in-residence" program that often exists in business or engineering schools. The relationship between Andrew Grove, former CEO of Intel, and the City College of New York is a well-known example of this approach. On our own campus, we have extended the entrepreneur-in-residence concept to include the medical school, as well as the departments of economics, chemistry, and policy studies.

Qualified alumni are available to fill this role at virtually any research university to the extent departments are willing to provide "room" for them. The impediment to the entrepreneurial residency is typically not a lack of funds, as many of the most qualified entrepreneurs are willing to work, at least on a part-time basis, for a relatively low salary so long as they are free to continue at least some of their activities outside of academia. Opposition comes from some who are slow to recognize the importance of entrepreneurial thinking and reluctant to include entrepreneurs as colleagues. Our experience is that once this opposition is overcome, the results are immediate and dramatic. An entrepreneurial voice amidst a group of talented scientists often leads to high-impact, entrepreneurial science.

Enterprise Creation

Enter the office of a university president and you see the portrait of the founder, perhaps a framed degree, sports mementos, and some photographs of the current occupant with a Nobel Prize winner or U.S. president. In addition to a large desk and a flat-screen computer terminal, there are several comfortable sofas covered in the school colors with drapes to match. The walls are lined with bookshelves filled with enticing titles from a variety of disciplines, and everything is arranged neatly, including the files on the mahogany desk. No matter how many of these offices you enter or how hard you search, you will be hard pressed to find a Lucite cube commemorating an initial public offering or a framed agreement for the licensing of university technology. Buildings are not named for university presidents based on the number of companies created during their tenures, and presidents are not remembered for the amount of licensing revenue generated during their years in office. Enterprise creation is seldom viewed as central to the mission of a research university. However, we believe enterprise creation is increasingly important both as an independent activity and as an indicator of the impact of a university on its region, the country, and the world. If a university is effectively attacking the world's biggest problems, then enterprises of all kinds will inevitably be a byproduct of the effort.

A better place to look for the Lucite cubes and framed licenses celebrating commercial success is the technology transfer office. Tech transfer is usually a group of small offices or cubicles, and the desks are piled high with thick files of patent applications, license agreements, and memoranda from the university counsel. Sitting at the desks are young professionals trained as scientists or engineers who have become adept at evaluating the commercial potential of technology of all kinds. They look tired because the office is chronically understaffed and overworked. They are almost always on the telephone mediating between university professors who are convinced their discovery will be worth at least a billion dollars, university administrators who want the institution to get its fair share in the unlikely case that the professor is correct, and outside business interests convinced it is impossible to enter into a commercially viable relationship with a major research university. It wouldn't be unusual for the head of the office to be huddled in a small conference room, meeting with several university trustees or alumni who have ideas about how technology transfer should reorganize itself to generate more revenue from intellectual property created by the university. You might find the Lucite cubes you are looking for displayed on a shelf in the biggest office in the suite but only because tech transfer effectively accomplished the second function in its name, "transfer."

When research undertaken by a university employee results in an idea with commercial applicability, tech transfer gets involved to protect the intellectual property that has been created, often by filing a patent, to establish the relative commercial rights of the inventor and the university, and to create an avenue for commercial development by licensing the invention to a third party or creating a spin-out corporation. While the office might serve an educational function in encouraging innovation, tech transfer usually gets involved at the end of the process once an idea has been created and has become a candidate for an enterprise. Despite efforts to assess and reward tech transfer based on the number of patent applications and the amount of revenue generated, the office has little influence on determining the kind of research universities do. In reality, this office most often gets involved long after a climate for impactful research has been created — yet, paradoxically, tech transfer is often held accountable for the results of that process.

The halls of the engineering school, home of the research and development that leads to those conversations in the tech transfer office, are quite different. There, one group of students is discussing a project to design a biodegradable stent to reduce the risk of infection. Another group is evaluating the merits of a summer internship with a green-tech start-up. A third is making plans to rehearse its project pitch for an upcoming sustainable enterprise business plan competition. Farther down the hall, you pass a laboratory where a multidisciplinary team is completing work on the design of a virtual lung. When you arrive at the dean's office, you notice a poster advertising a round-table discussion led by an engineering professor who has started two biotech companies. In the waiting room, there is a glass case filled with Lucite cubes. An administrative assistant behind a well-worn desk greets you. When asked whether all of those projects commemorated in Lucite began in the engineering school, the assistant laughs and says, "Of course not, but engineering gets involved in almost every big science project that goes on at the university."

A visit to the engineering school reminds us that, notwithstanding the enormous potential of universities as innovation engines that drive economic development and enterprise creation, optimizing that potential requires a focus on culture as well as execution. The conversations that take place in an academic community have the potential to impact enterprise creation far more than a technology transfer office or a set of rules and regulations. But it is not just the subject matter of the dialogue that is important; who is participating is important as well. Are there participants who like to make things as well as those who like to discover things? Are there contributions from people who spend part of their life outside academia to bring a broader perspective to the conversation? Do those around the table represent different ways of looking at the world and different life experiences? Is solving big problems considered core to the mission of the institution, and is success in this area routinely supported and even celebrated? And most important, is enterprise creation supported and encouraged at the highest levels of university leadership? We are persuaded that some universities have accomplished this much better than others. The chancellor of MIT, Phillip Clay, told us that innovation and entrepreneurship "are in the DNA" of his institution.[1] At Stanford, the campus appears united around the mission of solving great problems. We believe what we call the "translational disciplines" are key to encouraging a culture and a conversation that leads to enterprise creation.

What Are Translational Disciplines?

In an academic community, wherever we see new enterprises being created there is almost always a discipline involved that straddles the border between academia and the outside world. Faculty from translational disciplines often spend time each week engaged in enterprises outside the academy. The curricula teach hard skills, and professors and practitioners work together to prepare students for professional work. Internships and other forms of experiential learning are encouraged. These disciplines apply academic knowledge to real-world problems with an eye toward the customers, patients, clients, and readers who will ultimately help determine success.

The most obvious example of a translational discipline is engineering. As Jim Plummer, the dean of the Stanford School of Engineering, told us, "Engineers are translators; while scientists are discovering what is, engineers are creating what never was."[2] Unlike other disciplines, the focus in engineering is on building things without regard to where the idea for the "thing" originated. Plummer also told us his school identifies the world's biggest problems and then assembles teams to "go after them."

Engineers turn new ideas into practical solutions. Because this translational notion is so fundamental to the discipline, it influences everything from research to tenure decisions. While involvement in enterprises outside of the academy is merely permitted in most disciplines, in engineering it is deemed essential because such involvement informs teaching and research and helps professors, according to Plummer, "learn what the problems are." Outside involvement even helps engineering professors achieve tenure because engineering research is typically judged by its impact, and interaction with emerging enterprises is one important avenue to high-impact research. Enterprise creation is a fundamental part of the culture of engineering. It permeates the conversations that take place in the halls and in the classrooms. Experienced entrepreneurs are typically members of the engineering faculty and practicing entrepreneurs are frequent lecturers and guests. Since the engineering curriculum is essentially translational in nature, the skills associated with enterprise creation fit naturally, and courses can logically be designed that address it in detail. Most important, engineers define themselves as facilitators and team builders, and therefore they naturally reach out to other parts of the university to translate the big ideas of others into reality.

Engineering schools are logical catalysts for enterprise creation. But there are other disciplines and schools that also can play an important role in this process. Some universities, Harvard being an example, without a school of engineering have filled the void with a department or school of applied science that performs many of the same functions. Typically housed in the college or school of arts and sciences, this department has close ties to chemistry, physics, and biology, and has been known to morph over time into an engineering school or a hybrid engineering and applied sciences school (as at Harvard) or department. On some campuses, applied science has become the catalyst for enterprise creation. Other variants along the same line involve departments of materials science that have an emphasis on translation and enterprise creation. Multidisciplinary centers focus on a particular problem such as global warming, and hybrid disciplines such as biomedical engineering can serve a similar function. All have the potential to create a translational culture both within their own walls and throughout the university.

The business school represents another translational discipline and can play an important role in enterprise creation either in partnership with engineering or, when engineering is absent, in its place. Like engineering, the business school is deeply involved in the world outside of academia, viewing the commercial and civic sectors as "clients" and paying great attention to the needs of those who might employ its graduates. And many business schools prepare graduates to make a job rather than take a job. The curriculum itself teaches the skills required to create new enterprises. Executive MBA programs, an important element of the financial model of most business schools, bring practicing executives to campus on a regular basis, many of whom play an important role in shepherding big ideas into viable enterprises. A subculture exists within many business schools that can potentially spread to the greater university and lead the process of enterprise creation. We use the term "subculture" because the applied orientation of engineering is not as obvious in the academic discipline of business. Academic success is often tied to publication in journals read primarily by academics. Moreover, the culture in many business schools often isolates them from the larger university community. For example, Harvard Business School did not participate in Harvard's last university-wide fundraising campaign. Even the business school campus itself is often physically distant from the center of the main campus. All of this can be overcome, and, with the appropriate leadership, the business school can become a critical element, or even a leader, of enterprise creation at a research university.

There are other, less obvious candidates to play a leadership or supporting role in enterprise creation; they are the other translational disciplines on campus. Medicine is one possibility, especially in light of the growing convergence of the traditional sciences with computational science in pursuit of solutions to complex problems in human health. In the same way engineering and business schools have connections to commercial and civic enterprises, the medical school is connected to patients, and this connection brings critical insights into many of the fastest-growing areas of university research. In the future, the medical school may have the potential to perform the function of an engineering school when it comes to enterprise creation focused on human health. The emerging field of translational medicine is evidence of this opportunity. Other schools with this kind of potential include pharmacy, law, journalism, public health, and nursing. Each, if encouraged, can play a role in enterprise creation, and they can potentially combine to form an ecosystem or culture that embraces this activity on a university-wide basis.

Translational Disciplines Drive Enterprise Creation

With respect to engineering, enterprise creation is a fundamental byproduct of the discipline itself. Building enterprises is one of the things engineers do. Many business students want to start a company at some point in their careers, and they want to learn how to do it while in school. An increasing number of students in the other professional schools also aspire to participate in enterprise creation at some point. The desire to build businesses—to create products, deal with customers, and identify "cool" problems to solve—is part of the culture that pervades the translational disciplines. In universities where this culture reaches outside the walls of a particular school to impact the culture of the greater university, the results are dramatic. MIT alumni have started more than 5,000 companies, such as Intel, Bose, and Texas Instruments. MIT-related start-ups employ over a million people and account for over $230 billion in annual sales.

Because translational disciplines have, as part of their mission, prepared students for specific roles in the workforce (engineering and the professions), their culture fosters an ongoing dialogue between academics and practitioners. Students routinely engage in internships as part of the curriculum. Practitioners teach classes. Professional education is an important part of the curriculum. Together this creates a natural flow of ideas and perspectives that encourage the creation of enterprises. When a good idea comes up at lunch among a mix of practitioners, academics, and students, the conversation naturally turns to whether the idea could become a successful enterprise.

In translational disciplines, enterprise creation often informs research, and in some cases forms the basis for research. *The Venturesome Economy* by Columbia Business School professor Amar Bhide is an example of this. In advancing a theory suggesting the likely impact of India and China on the prosperity of the West, Bhide relies upon over twenty years of research on new and emerging businesses in the United States and India. The latter stages of his work focus exclusively on enterprises created or backed by venture capitalists. Similarly, in their book *Innovation—The Missing Dimension*, Richard Lester and Michael Piore, professors at MIT, develop a set of ideas about innovation and new product development. The book is based on their work at the MIT Industrial Performance Center, where they studied cell phones, medical devices, and apparel—all areas ripe for innovation and, ultimately, new enterprise creation. When faculty can advance professionally by studying and understanding activities that lead to new enterprise creation, it profoundly impacts the culture and the conversations in which they participate. Enterprise creation becomes fundamental, not peripheral, to the professional development of many academics in the translational disciplines.

It is hard to overestimate the impact of an entrepreneur on the worldview of an engineering or business student. There is simply no substitute for spending time with people who have the passion and the perseverance to create something new. Whether it is Wendy Kopp discussing the "dark years," as she calls them, when it was unclear whether Teach for America was going to make it, or Jud Bowman, a twenty-four-year-old entrepreneur who gave up a full scholarship to Stanford in order to found PinPoint Technologies, the heat in the classroom goes up when someone who has "done it" arrives. Students take notes not because they are concerned the material will appear on a final exam but because they are getting real-world insights that complement their academic training. Any question about the impact of guest speakers is answered at the end of the class when speakers are inevitably deluged with additional questions. Infusing a start-up mentality into the curriculum through the free flow of faculty between the classroom and start-ups of all kinds only adds to the richness of the classroom experience.

Involvement in the process of creating new enterprises is also a rich learning experience for students in the translational disciplines, and, notwithstanding the unpredictability of such an experience, many students characterize internships and consultancies with start-ups as among the best learning experiences of their college or graduate school career. In our experience, entire classes based around enterprise creation and culminating in participation in a business plan competition have proven to be an ideal way to marry theory and practice—to stimulate the drive and passion required to do something new. Just as a scientist needs experience in the laboratory in order to understand the lessons of the classroom, students in the translational disciplines need practical experience and involvement. The creation of an enterprise is an ideal vehicle for providing such experience.

Turning an idea into a reality, whether it is a scientific discovery, a global health initiative, or an interdisciplinary institute, takes a set of specific skills that are not broadly taught and practiced in academia. They are, however, very much resident in the translational disciplines, especially engineering and business. The skills required include strategy, design, product development, marketing, finance, and execution. In an ideal world, the schools of engineering and business would combine forces and become key contributors to campus enterprise creation. We know of only a few instances where this has actually happened. More typically, specialized workshops, seminars, and business plan competitions are offered or organized by one school or department with limited outside participation. Moreover, the purpose of these activities is usually to educate a particular group of students and not to encourage enterprise creation campus-wide. The ultimate structure of such an effort is less important than the recognition that the core competencies required for enterprise creation are not typically available on a university campus. Without a concerted and focused effort led by at least one of the translational disciplines, those core competencies will not be cultivated to any significant degree.

Alumni from translational disciplines want to be involved in enterprise creation and are in a position to make a significant impact. Experienced entrepreneurs are delighted with the opportunity to work on campus-based ideas. In fact, most schools and departments that solicit alumni for this function report they have more interest than they can employ, and their network of graduates with start-up expertise is among their greatest assets. The challenge is to connect these alumni to projects throughout the university without regard to departmental boundaries. An entrepreneur and an academic combining to found a new enterprise is a theme we have discussed throughout this book. Facilitating this process in a systematic way will, we are convinced, give a huge impetus to campus-wide enterprise creation. Engaging alumni in enterprise creation has the added benefit of gaining commitment for the work of the university and providing a pathway for long-term financial support. There is no substitute for the kind of deep involvement that this process demands. At the end of the process, alumni will almost certainly have a deeper commitment and greater enthusiasm for what goes on inside the university.

When engineering, business, or other professional schools engage with the campus at large, the conversation changes and enterprise creation is often a topic of discussion. At places such as MIT, Stanford, and Babson College, where enterprise creation is expected, conversations naturally turn to opportunities, resources, and ventures and involve representatives across the campus. However, at traditional research universities, the translational disciplines too often remain in silos, removed from the heart of campus and with limited impact on the conversations that shape the university community. Active participation of schools such as engineering and business in the university at large also changes the institutional agenda. It provides a unique perspective on which problems should be attacked, and where to begin. The challenge is to find ways to encourage this sort of engagement. What follows are a few examples that have worked.

The Stanford Summer Institute for Entrepreneurship

Graduate and postdoctoral students from a variety of disciplines are interested in learning the skills required for enterprise creation. Chemists want to understand what it takes to start a biotech company. Public health students are interested in sustainable enterprises as a means of attacking disease. Medical students are interested in the opportunity afforded by bridging the gap between clinical knowledge and commercial applications. Journalists gravitate to the opportunities afforded by the demise of the newspaper and the rise of new media. However, their core disciplines traditionally have neither the capability nor the inclination to teach innovation, entrepreneurship, and enterprise creation.

Professor Garth Saloner and his colleagues at the Stanford Business School have addressed this challenge by creating the Stanford Summer Institute for Entrepreneurship. Established in 2007, this month-long, ungraded summer program involves roughly seventy masters-level, doctoral, and postdoctoral students primarily from engineering, medicine, and the natural sciences. Students need not have a project they want to develop in order to apply, but most of them do. Morning sessions are led by faculty from the Stanford Business School and employ lectures and the case method to teach the basics of finance, strategy, marketing, intellectual property protection, negotiation, company formation, and other hard skills. Afternoons involve outside speakers, networking, and working on a business plan in a team setting. The business plans, based on ideas advanced by students, are presented to a panel of outside judges at the end of the institute.

According to Professor Saloner, the program attracts incredibly bright students who learn the basics very fast. What is most exciting, he says, is when students combine their areas of expertise with what they learn in class. One student group conceived of a medical device to detect the symptoms of an imminent stroke and is exploring ways of making the device widely available. Another group invented an external sound-emitting system for quiet, fuel-efficient vehicles so that pedestrians can be warned of their approach. This team is exploring ways to market their system to manufacturers and owners. A third student group focused on how to launch a technological and entrepreneurial training center in rural Uganda. The institute arms extraordinary students with a set of skills and a way of thinking about innovation and then gives them a chance to employ those skills in the planning and creation of an enterprise. It is an excellent model to involve a translational discipline in a university-wide effort to encourage entrepreneurship as part of graduate education.

The Deshpande Center at MIT

At MIT, enterprise creation is purposeful and systematic, and one example of how this is actually accomplished is the Deshpande Center, whose stated mission is to increase the impact in the marketplace of technology developed at MIT. Since 2002, the center has funded more than eighty projects with more than $9 million in grants. Eighteen of them have evolved into commercial ventures that have collectively raised more than $140 million in outside financing from thirteen venture capital firms.[3] The center has provided support to a range of emerging technologies including biotechnology, biomedical devices, information technology, new materials, nanotech, and energy innovations. Although commercial impact is the stated goal, the center's director, Charles Cooney, says that the criteria for picking technologies involves not only potential commercial impact but academic and social impact as well. Although enterprise creation is one of the possible outcomes of the center's work, the organization also explores commercial licenses and other avenues to commercialization.

Over the past seven years, the Deshpande Center has developed a unique approach to commercializing technology. First, the center does not support projects that Cooney characterizes as incremental. He told us, "If there is incremental benefit from the innovation, it's probably going to happen anyway, and it doesn't need the kind of catalytic support the Deshpande Center provides."[4] Second, the center funds research projects, not companies. Third, all grant recipients are assigned a mentor from the entrepreneurial community to provide insight into the market opportunities available to the technology. These mentors are volunteers, typically graduates of MIT working in private industry. Their role is to serve as a catalyst, or as Cooney characterizes it, "to accelerate the translation of the technology to reach impact."[5] More specifically, mentors focus on market uncertainty with an eye toward understanding whether the technology will achieve some level of interest from commercial enterprises and ultimately from end users. Mentors are not permitted to participate directly in the formation of a company that may result from the project. If they choose to participate in such a manner, they must give up their role as advisor to the grant recipient. Cooney reports there is no shortage of qualified mentors willing to take on this role.

The process of identifying research projects begins with a simple three-page proposal based on a form available on the center's website. Over the years, more than 400 proposals have been submitted. The idea is to make the initial submission simple so a wide variety of researchers will participate. In any yearly review cycle, roughly thirty-five initial proposals are received and a review panel made up of entrepreneurs, venture capitalists, and academics determines which applicants should prepare a full proposal and presentation. In the second round, a different panel made up of academics selects proposals to receive a one-year, $50,000 "ignition" grant, with the understanding that if sufficient progress is achieved the project may receive an additional grant of up to $250,000 in the second year. Projects are funded for only two years because it is expected that within that time period the commercial potential will be demonstrated, and continuing funding will come either from outside investors, a licensing agreement, or some other commercial arrangement.

Cooney reports that, for the scientists who apply, the opportunity to work with a mentor and with a group of MIT students called an I-Team is as important as the monetary grants. University scientists are most excited about connecting with the possible markets for their research, interacting with the business and venture capital communities, and involving MIT students from business and engineering in their efforts to understand the potential commercial applications for their research. In most cases, the grant applicants have other avenues for funding their research but little access to the unique resources and approach the Deshpande Center brings to commercialization and enterprise creation. Not surprisingly, the center is deeply involved in what Cooney calls the "ecosystem" of entrepreneurship at MIT. Although based in engineering, the center cooperates closely with the business school and reaches out to all parts of the institution for research proposals. It carefully considers the academic and social implications of its grants with an eye toward furthering publication and social impact, as well as commercial acceptance. The Deshpande Center is both a product of the culture of innovation and entrepreneurship that characterizes MIT and a catalyst for the critical conversation that must take place at any entrepreneurial research university.

Stanford Technology Ventures Program

Whenever the conversation turns to entrepreneurship education, especially in engineering and the sciences, Tom Byers and the Stanford Technology Ventures Program (STVP) will likely come up. Byers was a pioneer when, in the mid-1990s, he adapted for the Stanford School of Engineering a curriculum on entrepreneurship created in the nation's leading business schools. He was well suited for the task. His own career spans the worlds of theory and practice, as he has worked in large and small commercial enterprises as well as obtaining a Ph.D. in management from the Haas School at the University of California, Berkeley. Byers also worked with a number of high-tech enterprises and knows the potential waiting to be unlocked in engineering and the sciences. In his view, innovation and entrepreneurship is too important an opportunity to be left solely to any one school. In the years since its founding, STVP has gone from a few isolated courses in the School of Engineering's Department of Management Science to a comprehensive undergraduate and graduate curriculum that integrates rigorous academic study. Byers has coauthored a popular textbook on high-tech entrepreneurship and combines the academic rigor he brings to the classroom with the insight provided by professionals from nearby Silicon Valley. These professionals participate in the curriculum both as guest lecturers who bring real-world expertise to his classes and as full- and part-time faculty members. Students in STVP courses now come from all parts of the university, and the speaker series the program sponsors is almost always standing room only. STVP receives substantial support from the surrounding high-technology community, and this human and financial capital results in the participation of entrepreneurial leaders from all over the world. In a typical week, representatives of billions of dollars of venture capital interact with CEOs of budding start-ups. Two notable companies that sprang from Stanford are Google and Symantec. Enterprise creation is at the heart of the conversations that take place at STVP, and, according to Byers, the help of President John Hennessy has made enterprise creation central to the culture of the engineering school and the university at large.

One of the most interesting facets of STVP is the Mayfield Fellows Program, designed to give twelve students a year an intensive theoretical and practical understanding of the techniques for growing technology companies. Enrollment, which is highly competitive, is open to undergraduates from any discipline, and the one-year curriculum combines a sequence of courses on managing technology ventures with a paid internship at a start-up company and mentoring from leading Silicon Valley luminaries. The results of the program are remarkable. Alumni now populate start-up and established companies throughout Silicon Valley as well as important nongovernmental organizations (NGOs) and venture capital firms. Although precise data is not available, a back-of-the-envelope calculation indicates alumni are involved in early-stage ventures representing hundreds of millions of dollars in market capitalization.

Recently, there has been a shift at STVP. Teaching entrepreneurship to engineers and others on campus is now set in the context of solving the world's biggest problems. The engineering school plays an important role as a bridge between disciplines. In fact, Byers recently stated the new focus of his personal efforts is to get much more involved with academics outside of engineering in an effort to bring the core competencies developed at STVP to the Stanford campus at large. Such efforts can only result in a still-wider conversation on enterprise creation and give additional energy to the enterprise-creating potential of the Stanford community.

Launching the Venture

The programs we have discussed thus far encourage enterprise creation either by teaching entrepreneurial skills to those in a position to start something new or encouraging research that has commercial potential. Such programs are directed at exposing students to the opportunity, teaching specific skills, and providing practical experience. Launching the Venture, a joint program of the Kenan-Flagler Business School at the University of North Carolina and the university's Office of Technology, takes a more direct approach, focusing on those ready to start an enterprise. The year-long course is open to students, faculty, and staff at the university. It is aimed at participants committed to launching a venture, whether it is a commercial business or a social enterprise. Established in 2004 as an offshoot of a technology commercialization course, the program has involved more than 500 participants and launched more than eighty ventures in the course of its existence. Projects range from high-tech start-ups founded by eminent professors to Internet retailing sites formed by undergraduates. Participants in the program are accepted after an application process designed to determine the likelihood that the proposed project, with the proper support, can actually be launched. The applicants are also screened for the personal qualities necessary to turn an idea into a reality. Approximately thirty-two teams are accepted each year, and within the second weekly session each team is assigned at least one coach with both entrepreneurial experience and domain expertise. The content of the class involves lectures, functional workshops, and lab sessions combined with hands-on, expert coaching. Business students are recruited to work with teams that need a particular skillset, such as marketing, financial planning, or management, and other interdisciplinary combinations are encouraged. Many of the projects enter the Carolina Challenge, a campus-wide idea competition that takes place each spring and awards $50,000 in prize money. Because the program involves both the business school and the technology development office, the curriculum is rooted in practicality and focused on creating viable enterprises of all kinds.

The class is organized in three phases. In phase one, which lasts seven weeks, market feasibility is examined to determine whether the idea is viable—whether there is a market or other means of support that has the potential to provide a sustainable revenue stream. At the end of this phase, each team presents its project to a panel to determine which projects demonstrate the potential to move forward. Approximately half the teams are picked to continue to the second phase on strategy. This phase also lasts seven weeks and is designed to create a detailed strategic plan focusing on the activities that make each enterprise different and can provide a sustainable comparative advantage. At the end of the second phase, the projects are evaluated again, and those that have successfully formulated a unique approach move on to the third phase, which focuses on the numbers, including detailed financials and a funding plan, and includes the formulation of a detailed timeline for obtaining the start-up financing required for launch. At the end of phase three, the teams are ready to begin the launch process. Close to 90 percent of the teams that complete the course, on average, actually implement their project. This focused approach to enterprise creation was recognized in 2006 as the best new business launch course in the country by the National Consortium of Entrepreneurship Centers.

4

Social entrepreneurship is one of the most powerful and important ideas to emerge in our society in recent years, and it is having a dramatic impact on every major university. A decade ago, the term was known only to a few theoreticians and isolated groups of enlightened idealists; just over five years ago an article in the *New York Times* describing the new field was considered to be groundbreaking.[1] Today, a Google search of the term results in 1.3 million hits, and tens of thousands of nongovernmental organizations now characterize themselves or their founders as "social entrepreneurs." Influential commentators characterize the movement as the wave of the future—a compelling and effective means of employing philanthropic resources of all forms. Those who believe the research university must attack the world's biggest problems cannot ignore this remarkable movement. Its development illustrates a central thesis of this book: when entrepreneurship is added to a mix that already includes significant financial and human resources and passion, remarkable things can happen.

The desire to heal the world and make things better is as old as civilization itself. By the turn of the nineteenth century, the idea of "scientific charity" emerged. The idea was that "modern" principles in health, education, and commerce could usefully be applied to the plight of the poor. The work of Florence Nightingale, the Boy Scouts and Girl Scouts, and Goodwill Industries are popular examples of the results of this movement. Still, the word "entrepreneurship" was seldom expressly associated with the impulse to "change the world," although Andrew Carnegie, in his essay "The Gospel of Wealth," paved the way. That changed in the late 1990s when the idea that entrepreneurship could have broad implications for the social sector began to take hold. Lord Young of Dartington, one of Britain's foremost social entrepreneurs, founded the School for Social Entrepreneurs in 1998. At around the same time, Bill Drayton, an early leader in the movement, began to characterize his Ashoka Fellows, a group committed to solving the world's most pressing problems through systematic change, as "social entrepreneurs" with the potential to bring about significant social change in a country or a multinational region. Large philanthropic funds and foundations began to emerge with "social entrepreneurship" as their mission. In fact, Ashoka's 1998 annual report was entitled "Leading Social Entrepreneurs." Words such as *sustainability* and *accountability* became central to the missions of organizations of all kinds that aspire to make a positive difference in the world. These groups wanted to go beyond the traditional donor-NGO relationship, to think more creatively, and to bring innovation to the process of social change. Most significant, high-visibility entrepreneurs began to employ their skills in activities, both nonprofit and for profit, to effect substantial social changes. The revelation that doing well and doing good need not be mutually exclusive led many in both sectors to believe that profit-seeking ventures could have an important role in addressing vast problems. The line between the private sector and the civic sector began to blur. What had begun as an obscure idea quickly emerged as a full-fledged social movement.

What Is Social Entrepreneurship?

Like the definition of entrepreneurship itself, a definition of social entrepreneurship is elusive. It is difficult to capture in the definition the breadth and power of the concept without making it so inclusive that it loses its meaning. We will begin with a specific example of a social entrepreneur and then work backward toward a general definition. In 2006, Muhammad Yunus became the world's best-known social entrepreneur when he received the Nobel Peace Prize. Yunus grew up in Bangladesh and was trained in the United States as an economist and banker. He returned home to serve as a government bureaucrat and sought to establish a factory in his spare time. In 1976, Yunus encountered a group of forty-three women in the small village of Jobra who scratched out a subsistence making bamboo furniture, but most of their income went to pay interest on usurious loans. Yunus lent the women twenty-seven dollars out of his own pocket and guaranteed them a larger loan if the initial loan was repaid.

These were the humble beginnings of what would become Grameen Bank. Yunus believed that placing lending decisions in the hands of small organized groups like the women in Jobra would dramatically increase the likelihood of repayment. The concept quickly expanded to other "unbankable" groups typically thought to be beyond the reach of any conventional financial institution. Over time, the practice became known as "microcredit," and it has taken hold in virtually all parts of the developing world. The Grameen Bank itself has lent more than $6.38 billion to 7.4 million borrowers. The same basic principles used to found Grameen Bank have been employed to establish Grameenphone, the largest private telephone company in Bangladesh. A number of other enterprises aimed at providing goods and services to the poorest members of Bangladeshi society have followed suit.

In its citation, the Nobel Prize committee characterized Muhammad Yunus as someone who "translated visions into practical actions for the benefit of millions of people," and these words might also characterize a successful social entrepreneur. Yunus tested and applied concepts originally enunciated by Akhtar Hameed Khan, founder of the Pakistani Academy for Rural Development. Most of Yunus's for-profit and nonprofit enterprises are self-sustaining despite requiring initial support from government or other outside sources. Yunus was driven to dramatically reduce poverty in one of the poorest countries in the world, and he applied principles learned as an economist and banker to create a practical and sustainable business model that could be scaled to encompass the entire country. His original concept involved a dramatic innovation: the notion that very small loans could be made successfully to very poor people. Yunus's Grameen Bank not only brought capital—and ultimately goods and services—to underserved markets, but it also created new markets that did not exist until his innovative ideas revealed them. From the beginning, Yunus embraced market principles; he understood that unless loans were repaid, including a reasonable rate of return on the principal, he could not sustain and grow his vision.

Of course, there is only one Muhammad Yunus, but his story suggests the outline for a definition of social entrepreneurship. Peter Drucker reminds us that "entrepreneurship is by no means confined to economic institutions."[2] Duke University's Professor Gregory Dees,

one of the intellectual leaders of the social entrepreneurship movement, says social entrepreneurs reach across sectors to effectively address the world's biggest problems. Social entrepreneurs blend social
purpose with an entrepreneurial orientation. They value results over
good intentions and are not particularly concerned whether their
enterprises are for profit or nonprofit. They set clear goals, demand
accountability, and embrace built-in feedback mechanisms that routinely measure profit and loss. They believe in market-based solutions
but understand that not all projects can be sustained without outside support. Even self-sustaining enterprises need seed capital in the
form of grants and contributions. Social entrepreneurs innovate with
the relentless drive and enthusiasm common to all entrepreneurs,
and they employ many of the same skills that are required to succeed
in the commercial sector.

Why Is Social Entrepreneurship Important?

Social entrepreneurs will play a central role in responding to the challenges of the modern world, and we believe their presence will vastly
increase the impact research universities have in addressing these
problems. Aside from this lofty vision of the social entrepreneur's new
role, there are more practical reasons why embracing social entrepreneurship makes sense for a research university.

The first is that students are passionate about it. Idealism is alive
and well on college campuses, and there is evidence it currently thrives
at a level unprecedented since the late sixties. Teach for America
(TFA), a program that sends students from elite universities to teach
in urban settings, is the largest employer of recent graduates from our
campus, and 11 percent of the graduating class at Harvard applied to
the program in 2008. In 2004, young voters reversed decades of declin-
ing participation, and in 2008 they turned out in numbers not seen
since 1972. Professor Jeffrey Sachs, sometimes with the help of rock
star Bono, routinely draws standing-room-only audiences to hear him
talk about eliminating extreme poverty worldwide by 2015. Universities are responding to student activism with grants and tuition cred-
its for students who forgo lucrative employment immediately after
graduation in favor of lower-paying jobs that will improve the world.
Among students we have mentored over the last several years, many
are interested in dedicating their talents to social ends using modern
techniques such as social entrepreneurship. They have plans of their

own in this area and are anxious to acquire the skills necessary to turn their ideas into reality.

For example, after studying the history and current status of Teach for America, one of our classes drafted a strategic plan and presented it to TFA founder Wendy Kopp. Kopp engaged in a class discussion as to how TFA's success—and the impact of the program's teachers—ought to be measured. Our class offered a critique of Kopp's expansion strategy and suggested that obtaining critical mass in fewer school districts might make more sense than placing teachers in a larger number of districts.

In another class, after concluding that environmental remediation was an issue of critical importance, we had a session with Tom Darden, founder and CEO of Cherokee Investments, a private equity fund of nearly $2 billion focused on, among other things, brownfield remediation, with over 500 projects throughout North America and Europe. Cherokee purchases real estate unattractive to other buyers because of environmental problems, cleans up the sites, and sells or develops them for a profit. Our class used Cherokee's example to discuss strategy. Students wanted to understand the motivation of Cherokee's investors and the kind of return that was required in order to continue to attract capital. They also wanted to understand Cherokee's sustainable competitive advantage in light of the large number of copycat funds that were emerging. Ultimately, several new strategies emerged based on Cherokee's unique competencies, and at the end of class a group of students were anxious to pursue the discussion.

Gary Hirshberg, a lifelong environmentalist and CEO of Stonyfield Farm, the world's largest organic yogurt producer, suggested that for-profit enterprises would lead in addressing global warming. Hirshberg made it known that he was not devoting any of his own time or energy to enterprises addressing global warming that were not profit based. In a recent collaboration with Muhammad Yunus, Hirshberg arranged a partnership between the Danone Group (parent of the Dannon Yogurt Company) and Grameen Group to create a social business venture that would produce inexpensive dairy products in Bangladesh. The use of profit-generating models enables Hirshberg and Yunus to develop scalable and sustainable enterprises that can have a measurable impact on nutrition in Bangladesh and elsewhere.

There has never been a shortage of idealism on college campuses, but now idealists are beginning to embrace many of the principles of entrepreneurship. Measurable results are important. They do not discriminate between for-profit and nonprofit models to effect change. They are eager to make use of the tools employed by entrepreneurs—and they want to learn to think like entrepreneurs—but they have their own plans for making the world a better place.

The second reason for embracing social entrepreneurship on campus is that faculty respond to it. In fact, it can be the key to winning the hearts and minds of the faculty in the core disciplines at research universities. This was one of our premises at the beginning of our efforts to make entrepreneurship an important part of the intellectual fabric at UNC. The past five years have proven it to be true. We made Bill Drayton, a pioneer of social entrepreneurship and CEO of Ashoka, our first keynote speaker on entrepreneurship. Drayton has been laboring for thirty years to address the world's most difficult problems. In a series of meetings with faculty, students, and others, he described the efforts of Ashoka Fellows to create lasting social change and their realization that social change often requires entrepreneurial underpinnings in order to be sustainable. In essence, Drayton provided a seal of approval for the marriage of idealism and entrepreneurship that could not have come from those who could be perceived as having an agenda to bring entrepreneurship onto the campus. He also introduced a new way of communicating the tenets of social entrepreneurship that allowed academics of all stripes to embrace it as a practice consistent with their values.

The results of Drayton's visit were significant. An ongoing faculty seminar led by the chair of the faculty and attended by two other chairs was established. Serious scholarly research in anthropology grew out of that seminar. Ultimately, the university recruited an academic with research interests in social entrepreneurship. Departments began to compete to become the home for the social entrepreneurship curriculum. With respected senior faculty embracing entrepreneurship, younger faculty members were encouraged to join in. Though perhaps still a negative word to some, entrepreneurship had become a respectable topic of conversation, and thinking entrepreneurially was not only tolerated but encouraged by the university community. Social entrepreneurship was the key.

A third reason for advancing social entrepreneurship in the academy is that it offers an intellectual invitation for attacking big problems. In an institution like a research university, merely resolving to take on these challenges is usually not enough to foster more than a small number of unconnected, one-off projects funded by outside foundations or agencies. When the funding goes away, the projects disappear as well. A clear intellectual framework and vocabulary are required to make entrepreneurship a part of university culture. The field of social entrepreneurship offers a unifying structure that connects multiple departments and disciplines within the university. It also connects the university to other like-minded educational institutions, private foundations, and an emerging social movement.

Typically, the first step in effecting cultural change involves creating a social entrepreneurship curriculum—by no means a novel idea. Less than a decade ago Stanford founded a social entrepreneurship workshop to employ Silicon Valley principles to attack social problems. The workshop, which draws on schools as varied as design, law, and mechanical engineering, was founded partly in response to students who demanded assistance with projects important to them. Five years later, a similar workshop was offered at Harvard's Kennedy School as part of the Reynolds Foundation Fellowships in Social Entrepreneurship, which also included the Schools of Education and Public Health. By now, similar programs exist at many research universities. Occasionally the programs spawn small but important enterprises and projects. We would hasten to add that as social entrepreneurship grows and evolves, distinguishing it from entrepreneurship in general becomes more difficult. Certainly, the for-profit versus nonprofit distinction is no longer determinative; so many profit-making ventures have important social components. If a broad definition of entrepreneurship is adopted the need to carve out social entrepreneurship as a course of study separate from general entrepreneurship may not be necessary.

Early efforts to teach social entrepreneurship had an important effect on the burgeoning field of study. Pioneers in the field relied on a highly anecdotal approach, lacking academic rigor. The need to build a legitimate academic curriculum compelled innovative scholars such as Gregory Dees at Duke to begin to define social entrepreneurship more precisely and lay out an academic framework for faculty; simultaneously, an increasing number of successful programs were emerging in response to student interest. Powerful and influential new institutions such as the Gates Foundation began legitimizing and supporting social entrepreneurship as an important means of attacking great problems. Bill Gates summed up his foundation's new approach: "We have to find a way to make aspects of capitalism that serve wealthier people serve poorer people as well."[3] Jeff Skoll, the first president of eBay, endowed the Skoll Foundation with $250 million to support social entrepreneurship. Its mission statement reads as follows: "The Skoll Foundation's mission is to advance systemic change to benefit communities around the world by investing in, connecting, and celebrating social entrepreneurs. Social entrepreneurs are proven leaders whose approaches and solutions to social problems are helping to better the lives and circumstances of countless underserved or disadvantaged individuals."[4]

Klaus Schwab, the founder of the World Economic Forum, and his wife Hilde established the Schwab Foundation for Social Entrepreneurship in 1998. PBS aired an entire series dedicated to social entrepreneurship called *The New Heroes*, detailing the stories of twelve social entrepreneurs and the impact they are having on the world's big problems. Successful entrepreneurs such as Richard Branson, founder of Virgin Airways, and Pierre Omidyar, founder of eBay, have embraced the movement. The Skoll Centre for Social Entrepreneurship at Oxford University sponsors an annual conference, and social entrepreneurship has become an integral part of the World Economic Forum in Davos, Switzerland. Research in the field is becoming more widespread with support from organizations such as the University Network for Social Entrepreneurship. Most notably, a definitive anthology on social entrepreneurship, *New Models for Sustainable Social Change*, was published in 2007 by Dr. Alex Nicholls, Director of the Skoll Centre at Oxford.

A final argument for embracing social entrepreneurship on university campuses is that affluent donors will support it. While faculty and students are attracted to social entrepreneurship for idealistic reasons, entrepreneurs—a group of important potential donors for any university—are drawn to the idea because it embraces many of the principles that made them successful. Jeff Skoll, whose foundation grants over $40 million a year, was drawn to an entrepreneurial approach in which "the positive social returns vastly exceed the amount of time and money invested." Skoll's brand of philanthropy is "innovative, using the latest advancements to bring results."[5] The Skoll Foundation bequest to create the Skoll Centre for Social Entrepreneurship at Oxford was the largest gift ever given to a business school for such a purpose.

The Omidyar Network invested $110 million in 2008 in for-profit and nonprofit philanthropic enterprises. Omidyar believes that "sustainability, innovation, and scale . . . are critical to addressing the global challenges we face today."[6] When Omidyar became interested in microfinance, he and his wife, Pam, decided to help jumpstart the

movement by giving $100 million to Tufts University with the under-
standing that the gift would be invested in entities such as Muhammad Yunus's Grameen Bank. According to Tufts president Lawrence
Bacow, this gift would not have come to Tufts if there had not been a
willingness to undertake an investment strategy centered around new
financial institutions that have adopted a strategy for empowering the
poor through microloans. Omidyar was willing for the income from
his gift to be used for a broad range of projects at Tufts so long as the
corpus was invested in ways that were consistent with the Omidyar
microfinance strategy. On a much smaller scale, business schools at
Oxford, Harvard, Stanford, and Duke have all attracted donor support
for scholarship in social entrepreneurship.

The high-profile gifts by Skoll and Omidyar and the widespread
interest in social entrepreneurship among influential entrepreneurs
worldwide present a particularly attractive opportunity for research
universities. Social entrepreneurship is entering the mainstream, and
donors—especially entrepreneurial donors—will be increasingly willing to support the effort. The Skoll Centre serves as a model for what
can be done within a traditional academic framework, and there will
certainly be interest in moving beyond the business school (where the
Skoll Centre is housed) to other venues within the university. But there
is an opportunity here for doing more than just raising money. Social
entrepreneurship offers a framework and a vocabulary for engaging
important donors in the work of the university. Initially, entrepreneurs
want to contribute because the project is something they understand
and they have strong ideas about how it should be executed. As they
become more involved in execution, they grow more committed to the
effort and are therefore more likely to provide additional funds.

How Does It Work?

Having described the broad impact of social entrepreneurship on college campuses, we now turn to three specific examples.

MICROFINANCE AT TUFTS UNIVERSITY
Pierre Omidyar and his wife, Pam, are graduates of Tufts University.
Before Larry Bacow was installed as university president, the Omidyars were generous contributors, and both served the school in various capacities. Bacow, an economist from MIT, had ambitious plans
for the institution, beginning with a $1.2 billion fundraising campaign
called Beyond Boundaries. Few other universities had a pair of young

alumni as affluent as the Omidyars. When eBay went public in 1995, Omidyar was thirty-two, and his share of the company was estimated to be worth $1 billion. In early talks with Bacow, Omidyar made it clear that he considered funds invested as part of a large endowment to be "lazy capital." Large endowments often return a mere 5 percent of their value to the university every year; Omidyar wanted his money to have a more immediate impact.

After meeting with Muhammad Yunus and a group of influential Silicon Valley CEOs in November 2004, Omidyar saw the link between microfinance and his work at eBay. Both endeavors involved individuals "discovering their power" and facilitated social change.[7] The Silicon Valley CEOs calculated that it would take $65 billion to meet the capital requirements of a fully funded worldwide microlending effort as outlined by Yunus—a sum that could not be raised with a strictly philanthropic approach. But since microfinance had a proven track record of achieving a return on investment, Omidyar considered a different approach: everyone in the room would need to pledge 1 percent of their net worth (an amount they estimated to be $30 billion) to their alma maters with the understanding that the corpus was to be invested in microfinance and the income used in a manner satisfactory to the contributor and the institution.[8] There was interest in the plan, but the conversation quickly focused on technical matters that Omidyar could not answer. Everyone agreed that the plan was enticing, if only Omidyar could address the details.

Not surprisingly, Omidyar accepted the challenge and engaged Bacow in a conversation to find a way for his contributions to Tufts to be invested in the kind of microfinance activities spawned by Yunus and his disciples. The fact that he was willing to contribute $100 million to Tufts if the mechanics could be resolved added a certain urgency to the dialogue. Bacow knew Omidyar's proposition was a zero-sum game: either the institution determined how to make Omidyar's proposal work and got $100 million, or it got nothing.

Ultimately the Omidyar-Tufts Microfinance Fund (OTMF) was established as a separate tax-exempt legal entity. It derives its tax-exempt status by virtue of the control exerted by Tufts, but Omidyar and his advisor, Michael Mohr, participate as board members. Entrepreneurs have short time horizons, and Omidyar was eager to demonstrate the investment model. The OTMF mandate is to be fully invested within thirty-six months. Income and return from investments are split equally between reinvestment in the fund and expendable funds for Tufts. Because of the unpredictability of the returns, Tufts is dedicating its share to discretionary spending that can be scaled in either direction depending on the success of its investments.

Predictably, things have not gone exactly as planned, but many of the surprises have been good ones. Rather than indirect investments through other funds, direct investments, at least initially, have predominated. As a result, Tufts investment officers have developed valuable expertise in microfinance and view it as an alternative investment along the lines of venture capital or real estate. In fact, Bacow described the OTMF as a kind of venture capital fund for microfinance. At the moment, the fund is dealing with two countervailing developments. On the one hand, the field has become crowded, and not all of the players are looking for an investment-like return. On the other, microfinance itself is rapidly evolving from a small-loan model to a financial services approach that dramatically increases the kind and number of enterprises available for OTMF investment. Bacow is optimistic that some early investments may result in exceptional returns, but both he and Omidyar are certain there will be bumps along the way. Taking the attitude of a true entrepreneur, Omidyar said, "I'm sure we will learn a lot in the process."[9]

The OTMF has also had what Bacow calls "a transformative effect" on Tufts.[10] Faculty and students have become actively engaged in a variety of world problems through the Institute for Global Leadership. Research on microfinance has been funded through the Department of Economics and the profile of the school's commitment to social entrepreneurship has never been higher. The next several years will determine the dimensions and sustainability of the transformation Bacow describes, but there is little doubt Omidyar's fund will be viewed as a groundbreaking development for social entrepreneurship at a research university.

REDUCING TOBACCO USE AND JOHNS HOPKINS UNIVERSITY

For years, Michael Bloomberg has ardently campaigned against smoking. He has also been a loyal and generous supporter of Johns Hopkins University, serving as the chairman of its Board of Trustees and as a lead donor to the Bloomberg School of Public Health, generally acknowledged as the top school in the field. Bloomberg's unique understanding of the smoking issue and his appreciation of the resources of a university such as Johns Hopkins gave rise in 2005 to the multifaceted Bloomberg Initiative to Reduce Tobacco Use. Bloomberg's efforts exemplify an entrepreneurial mindset; from the outset, he sought to leverage the resources he contributed by involving a wide array of others in his effort. At Hopkins he reached beyond the School of Public Health to involve the Center for Communications Programs and departments of Epidemiology, Biostatistics, Environmental Health Sciences, Health Behavior and Society, and International Health. This team would have been ideal if research alone was what Bloomberg had in mind—but making a dent in worldwide tobacco use would take more than just research, and he knew it. Bloomberg commissioned a study led by the World Health Organization that concluded that the direct and indirect effects of tobacco make smoking the world's number one health hazard and contribute to scores of serious diseases. The study also established clearly defined milestones and metrics, another hallmark of entrepreneurial thinking, to measure the effects of the Bloomberg Initiative. Three other outside organizations were also recruited to the effort: the Centers for Disease Control and Prevention, the World Lung Foundation, and the Campaign for Tobacco-Free Kids. Bloomberg had the pieces in place and a plan for attacking the problem.

Bloomberg's initiative had been launched over a two-year period with the support of an initial grant of $125 million. But he was far from done. On July 24, 2008, Bloomberg and the Gates Foundation joined together to commit $500 million toward an effort called MPower which will implement the work of the Bloomberg antismoking initiative with special emphasis on China, Russia, India, Indonesia, and Bangladesh. Without question, Johns Hopkins has become the center of the universe when it comes to reducing tobacco use. Leaders from around the world attend its Institute for Global Tobacco Control Leadership Program. Five university departments and the School of Public Health have collaborated in the effort. Successfully employing an entrepreneurial approach, Bloomberg brought together a breathtaking array of financial and human resources to focus upon an important problem. He established clearly defined goals and identifiable metrics for success. This is exactly what we have in mind when we characterize entrepreneurship as the missing ingredient on university campuses. When it is added to an already-fertile mix, astounding things can happen.

ATTACKING WORLD HUNGER AT UNC

Kelly Fogelman, a medical student at the University of North Carolina, was doing health assessments at a Nicaraguan orphanage in the summer of 2000. Known as Los Chavalitos, the orphanage founded by Alehandro Obando serves twenty-two children and is located on a farm with a small staff and a few animals. Kelly's assessment revealed the children needed better nutrition than what was available. The answer was chickens. Thirty hens would produce enough eggs to feed the orphanage as well as generate revenue by selling the excess at a local market. But how does a financially strapped medical student provide the funds to buy nearly thirty chickens and construct a chicken coop? The solution came to be known as Hunger Lunch.

Like most entrepreneurial ideas, the basics of Hunger Lunch are simple. Donated food is used to provide UNC students with a rice-and-bean lunch at a minimal cost. The weekly lunches bring in money to support hunger-related programs and increase awareness of world hunger at the same time. Upon returning to school, Fogelman implemented the model by holding a Hunger Lunch twice a month at the UNC medical school. Food was supplied by the hospital cafeteria, a price of three dollars per plate was established, and student volunteers served the meals. At the end of the school year, profits amounted to about $2,500, enough to construct a chicken coop at Los Chavalitos and purchase thirty hens. Soon, those hens were laying twenty-five eggs per day, meeting the requirements of the orphanage and leaving a surplus of eggs to sell at the local market. Obando started a bank account with the profits and continued to use the money to finance and improve his operation.

With the model established, and with one year of experience, the question was could it be expanded? A sophomore premed student named Sindhura Citineni picked up the mantle. She heard Fogelman tell the Hunger Lunch story at a public service seminar and immediately saw the potential. At 3 A.M. the next morning, she came across an online map of the world with blinking lights. When a light blinks, it is because a person has died from malnutrition. Citineni had spent her eighth-grade year in India and had mental images of people in extreme poverty that she had seen but never talked to. That night "a switch went off." She wondered, "what if that [person in extreme poverty] was my dad," realizing that "he was someone's dad or brother."[11] The next day she met with the manager of Lenoir Hall, the campus dining center, and negotiated a deal. The rice, beans, and cornbread would be supplied for a dollar, and she would sell it for three. With $150 of her own money, Citineni launched Hunger Lunch on the main UNC campus and cleared $450 the first day—a sign that the model might have "legs."

The next step was to build an infrastructure that would move Sindhura's vision of a student-led attack on world hunger into a sustainable enterprise. She recruited a number of students to help her, and they entered a business plan competition for social ventures. One of her associates, Joel Thomas, emerged as her "inside operator" to complement her visionary leadership. The group quickly reached two conclusions: they wanted to turn Hunger Lunch into a national student organization, and they did not have the skills to do so. Not surprisingly, they decided to act on both propositions simultaneously. The organization was renamed Nourish International, and chapters were established on the campuses of Duke, North Carolina State, and Elon University. Weekly Hunger Lunches remained the cornerstone of the group's revenue-generating activities, and scores of students were sent each summer to work on hunger-related projects in Africa and Latin America. At the same time, Thomas and a number of his colleagues enrolled in the minor in entrepreneurship at UNC, and Nourish International became part of the campus Launching the Venture program (discussed in Chapter 3). Business models were conceived, debated, and reworked at the same time the organization was actually implementing its plan. At the heart of the discussions was the issue of sustainability: how could Nourish avoid the old donor model and create a series of activities that would consistently generate income to support its mission? The fundamental mission of the organization was also honed. Could Nourish truly have a measurable impact on world hunger, or should it focus more on providing college students with a life-changing experience that would, over time, build a national constituency for attacking the problem? Should the group focus only on a few projects and send all of their students each summer to work on them, or should each Nourish chapter sponsor its own project? Should revenue generation expand beyond Hunger Lunch, and, if so, what would be the next blockbuster?

These and other questions were explored and addressed over a two-year period. The group raised outside support to supplement Hunger Lunch and received prize money from competitions that it entered. In the summer of 2008, students from campuses throughout the United States came to Chapel Hill for a week-long program, and by fall there were Nourish chapters on twenty-three campuses, including Harvard, Yale, and Stanford. Predictably, the rapid growth has produced new challenges. Other events now complement Hunger Lunch as revenue generators, and each new chapter of the organization seems to have a twist on enhancing the top line. Sorting out the relationship between the national organization and the chapters is also a source of healthy dialogue. Interestingly, the discussion that began in the classroom of an introductory entrepreneurship class is framed in terms of "core competencies" and "value added," notions previously reserved for commercial activities. Now they have been embraced by students who want to change the world.

5

Multidisciplinary Centers

Making connections, encouraging conversations, and collaborating are essential elements of entrepreneurship,
and, increasingly, those activities have become critical to
the work of a research university in addressing the grand
challenges facing the world. The good news is that there is
seldom a shortage of proposals for the establishment of a
multidisciplinary center or some other configuration that
will readjust the traditional disciplines. The bad news is
that many of these proposals are incomplete at best and
wrongheaded at worst, and more often than not lack a plan
for sustainability. The challenge for the entrepreneurial
thinker is to harness what is essentially a productive development in academia and channel it toward long-term,
measurable results without creating more of the rigidity
and myopia that such centers were established to address.

The impetus for a multidisciplinary center usually comes
from one of two directions: from either the improvement
of research, teaching, and knowledge or the solving of one
or more important problems. The former, which might
be called "interdisciplinarity for its own sake," postulates
that if departmental silos are eliminated and scholars with
related interests are allowed to interact great things will
happen. The latter, which might be referred to as problem
driven, is often initiated by private donors or government
programs.

The push for interdisciplinarity in the name of improving the traditional work of the university has taken several

forms. Some institutions, centers, and schools were created to house scholars from disparate disciplines, with the conviction that encouraging dialogue or conversations across the disciplines will result in better teaching and scholarship. Examples of this approach include the hundreds of arts and humanities centers that have been created at colleges and universities nationwide. A second approach involves organizing a center or institute around a particular emerging area of knowledge such as biomedicine, new media, or human development. Again, there are examples of this approach at every major research university: Bio-X at Stanford, the Media Lab at MIT, and the Center for Human Development at the University of California, San Diego, are noteworthy examples. A third response is the creation of new departments or hybrid disciplines. Some, such as bioengineering and policy studies, have stood the test of time, while for others the jury is still out. The most radical approach is to "blow up" traditional departments entirely, replacing them with academic alignments that reflect fundamentally different organizational principles. At Arizona State University, President Michael Crow eliminated at least four traditional departments and replaced them with ten new schools or departments.

The other impetus for multidisciplinary programs and centers is to attack one or more big problems. Often, external funding is the precipitating event. Many such centers were originally funded by government grants or funding programs aimed at attacking issues determined to be important as a matter of public policy. For instance, the original seed money for the world-renowned Carolina Population Center (CPC) was a grant from the U.S. Agency for International Development (USAID), and today its core budget is provided by the National Institute of Child Health and Human Development (NICHD). Although the CPC is essentially a think tank for basic population research, its work influences population policy worldwide, often providing an intellectual framework for broad-based government or foundation initiatives. Large private foundations that are increasingly focusing their giving around a small number of global problems also can be the catalyst for the establishment of a center.

Individual donors, typically through their own private foundations, are the biggest drivers of problem-based centers. Each story sounds remarkably similar, but the results can be mixed. A wealthy donor becomes interested in a large problem and turns to his or her alma mater with the promise of a very large gift to enlist the university as a partner. The development office, eager to help the university meet endowment goals, welcomes the donor with open arms, and a faculty committee is established to respond. This dialogue can yield extraordinary results, such as the antismoking initiative centered in the Bloomberg School of Public Health at Johns Hopkins or the Skoll Center for Social Entrepreneurship at Oxford. And there are some well-documented failures as well, where donor intent and academic standards conflict or, worse still, where the problem the center was created to solve no longer merits the resources dedicated to it. Academia is not good at euthanasia, and as a result, such outmoded centers typically remain in existence, absorbing resources that could be used more productively elsewhere.

We should note that the establishment of a problem-driven center with funds from an individual donor can also unfold in a different, generally more desirable manner than that just described. The big problem is identified by the university through either a visionary leader or industrious faculty. Once an approach is developed, donors are identified to support the effort. Not surprisingly, this approach has been widely endorsed by academic committees and task forces. Stanford's Bio-X, the center we discuss later in this chapter, was founded in this manner.

Interdisciplinarity Is Here to Stay

Life is not divided into disciplines and neither are the world's biggest challenges. This is hardly a novel thought. In fact, over the last decade, it has been the centerpiece of countless reports, addresses, and academic papers. Two well-known academics described it this way: "Like a tsunami, emphasis on interdisciplinarity is the wave of the future; universities that have the foresight to now become prepared will have placed themselves in a position to make a difference in the years to come."[1]

The reasons are clear. Interconnections between the disciplines have become increasingly self-evident, and even basic cutting-edge research now requires tools, skills, and perspectives from multiple academic disciplines. Almost no important science is being done now without computational tools pioneered in computer science. Sophisticated medical research requires contributions from chemistry, biology, physics, and engineering. The same can be said of the social sciences, where, for instance, policy studies and economics have been converging for years, and sophisticated computer modeling is often as important to anthropologists as it is to economists. In the arts and humanities, studies of race, gender, and ethnicity involve contributions from humanists across campus, and "digital humanities" and "digital arts" are common descriptors. Significantly, the disciplines themselves and the departments and journals that rule them have also recognized that important research increasingly requires a multi-disciplinary approach. The chancellor of MIT, Phillip Clay, told us that almost no scientific research is done at his university without some collaboration with engineering. A similar sentiment was expressed by the dean of the Stanford School of Engineering, James Plummer, who also emphasized that tenure decisions in his department were made in large part based upon the impact of the research being undertaken. These days it can be hard to maximize impact when confined to a particular discipline or department.

External forces are also mandating interdisciplinary approaches. Government grants and private sector funding increasingly focus on problem-based research without regard to department or discipline. Public research universities are under constant political pressure to attack real-world problems rather than discipline-based basic research. Private foundations such as the Gates Foundation and others are focusing on discrete, important problems, and their grant making reflects those priorities. In fact, a consensus seems to be emerging as to the world's biggest problems. External funding sources will inevitably reflect this consensus.

In 2005, the Association of American Universities issued a document called "Report of the Interdisciplinarity Task Force," developed by a who's who of academia. The report characterized the growth of interdisciplinary cooperation as reflecting "the need for new combinations of disciplinary knowledge and research methods to solve new and complex problems."[2] The eighteen-page report goes on to outline best practices and approaches for implementing interdisciplinarity in higher education—a certain indicator that this trend will be with us for the foreseeable future.

Centers and Institutes Do Not Take the Place of Departments and Academic Disciplines

Michael Crow, president of Arizona State University, refers to himself as an academic entrepreneur. Crow has emerged as the poster child for the elimination of traditional academic departments and disciplines and their replacement with nontraditional centers. His reputation is well deserved. In his first six years at ASU, he eliminated or merged the departments of Sociology, Anthropology, Biology, and Geology and moved the Economics Department to the School of Business. At the same time he started ten new schools or departments such as Human Evolution and Social Change, Earth and Space Exploration, Family and Social Dynamics, Sustainability, and Life Sciences. In the process he hired twenty-one new deans, moved four colleges off campus, and added 15,000 students and 7 million square feet of space. Crow's vision of interdisciplinarity is a powerful one, and it may well be the correct approach for the rapidly evolving university he leads. However, for a preponderance of research universities, departments and academic disciplines will survive as fundamental organizational mechanisms.

In the first place, the disciplines provide the intellectual rigor required for effective problem solving of all kinds. The new ways of thinking required in the twenty-first century will be grounded in methods and approaches that can best be learned through a deep dive in a discipline such as economics or chemistry or history. Generally, the subject matter itself is not as important as the methods and concepts that can only be assimilated over many years of study and hard work. There is also an element of apprenticeship in working through the process. To become an economist you need to spend time with economists, and ideally you need a mentor or role model who teaches the elements of the profession not found in textbooks. Ultimately, interdisciplinary centers will not work without trained academics to do the work. These centers need economists and biologists and computer scientists and humanists; and they all have to be educated somewhere.

Traditional departments also provide an intellectual and administrative home for faculty that is difficult to replicate elsewhere. Their painstaking hiring processes, the almost-ritualistic university traditions governing tenure, and the extensive professional meetings, seminars, conferences, and publications all serve as a certification and continuing education process for academics. This is similar to the roles played by state bar associations or medical boards for lawyers and doctors. Departments handle the necessary administrative matters that accompany those responsibilities. Barbara Entwisle, the director of the Carolina Population Center, commented that avoiding the need to make hiring, salary, and tenure decisions frees her to focus on execution. "I like making things happen, not telling people what they can't do," she said.[3] With the certification issues taken care of, interdisciplinary centers can focus on different interlinked issues: What kind of team can best attack the problem at hand? What mix of disciplines will yield the most interesting research results? What kind of academic dialogue will suggest new and important approaches to the world's biggest problems?

Perhaps the best argument for the traditional disciplines and departments is that they provide a bedrock foundation for the academy and in so doing facilitate innovative academic groupings outside their boundaries. As any university administrator will tell you, it is hard to eliminate a department, especially at a research university. The traditions of collegiality, the impulse toward comprehensiveness, the need to compete with peers nationally, and the sheer inertia of large institutions make closing departments a daunting task. Michael Crow's breathtaking vision to the contrary, most university presidents have concluded that this is not the way to go.

On the other hand, centers and institutes don't have to last forever. They can begin as informal collaborations, evolve into programs or centers, and only when they prove their long-term viability become more permanent entities. If they outlive their usefulness, they can be closed down more easily than academic departments. The more permanent alignments offered by departments provide the stability that large institutions require and in a sense give permission for the innovation facilitated by centers, institutes, and other less formal interdisciplinary alignments.

We hasten to add that for all of this to work, the departments must be compensated for their contribution. This can be accomplished in a number of ways. Faculty time can be bought out for a semester or a year so long as the buyout is viewed as equitable and not an unfair burden on the department. A portion of the indirect costs generated by interdisciplinary grants can be remitted back to the departments of those who received the grants. This approach can make a center a welcome adjunct to a department, with the revenue it generates paying some or all of faculty salaries and the department also receiving additional funds in the form of overhead. Centers are wise to remit not only financial compensation but also credit for success back to the departments. When a faculty member or team achieves interdisciplinary success of any kind, the participating departments are to be acknowledged and their farsightedness in participating in academic innovation praised. Centers are often perceived as fashionable and therefore generate favorable press that traditional departments cannot duplicate. Sharing the limelight goes a long way toward solidifying the relationship between centers and departments. It is also important that centers stick to their mission and are not seen as encroaching on the role of the departments. Barbara Entwisle remarked that the Carolina Population Center's positive relationship with the School of Public Health developed because her center stuck to population research and resisted the push by outside funders to move into peripheral areas such as maternal and children's health, traditionally the purview of public health.

Interdisciplinarity Grows out of Demonstrable Collaboration

Bottom up works better than top down in most undertakings, and interdisciplinarity is no exception. Even when bold, innovative academic leaders create an interdisciplinary vision they are well advised to build their plan on activities that promise real results and have strong faculty support from the outset. In an era of scarce resources and increased demands for accountability, reshuffling the deck is not enough. Creating a center because it can attract grants and the accompanying overhead payments is not a winning, long-run strategy, and sophisticated funders will inevitably see through it.

This lesson has played out consistently as interdisciplinarity has gained momentum and credibility. At the University of California, San Diego, a program in human development was proposed by faculty in social science, biological sciences, and the arts and humanities, all of whom had an extensive history of previous collaboration. Eminent faculty were involved in the enterprise from the outset, and they were willing to devote significant time to the effort. The administration was willing to provide support for the program so that it was not viewed as coming at the expense of the departments. At the end of the day eleven separate departments and programs affiliated with the effort, and a new Ph.D. program in human development was approved in 2005. The University of Illinois's famed Beckman Institute, which supports research in biological and computer intelligence and electronic and molecular nanostructures and was initially conceived by university administrators, was ultimately based on proposals growing out of two collaborations: one between engineering and the physical sciences and another between life and biological sciences. At our own institution, the Institute for the Arts and Humanities (IAH), a powerful force for interdisciplinarity on campus, grew out of a small seminar among faculty from the College of Arts and Sciences, moderated by a religion professor and housed in a ramshackle house that was a candidate for demolition.

What does not work is the imposition of a grand vision for inter-disciplinarity without a requisite foundation of faculty cooperation. Examples abound but no one is anxious to discuss them. The story is often the same. An exciting vision is set forth for interdepartmental cooperation around an extraordinary problem. The rationale is clear because the departments and even the people involved are preeminent in their fields. In some cases a superstar is recruited to lead the effort. However, if there is no foundation for cooperation, the effort will fail. There are reasons for this: the targeted departments do not play well together or have conflicting priorities. Their faculty recruitment strategies are different, or there is simply not enough in it for the participating departments. In fact, fostering the requisite interdisciplinary cooperation to make a center or institute work is harder than raising the resources to fund it. Starting small, encouraging existing collaborations, and embracing temporary academic alignments is a winning approach to nurturing ongoing collaboration. Once it has taken root, building out a larger vision makes more sense.

Test Drive Before You Institutionalize

Establishing a center, school, or institute at a research university is typically daunting, involving approval from numerous committees and administrators and, most important, the commitment of a huge amount of dollars often in the form of endowment that will yield a relatively small percentage for annual operations. These slow, difficult processes are in place for a reason. Once established, these institutions take on a life of their own, and, as mentioned earlier, closing them becomes difficult. Ironically, many of the best ideas for interdisciplinary collaboration never get off the ground because they start too big, and by the time the stars have aligned, the leadership has moved on to other things, the focus of the proposed enterprise has changed, or potential donors have lost interest. An alternative is to think entrepreneurially and demonstrate the viability of the enterprise using relatively small amounts of expendable funds and resources volunteered by relevant departments. Involving potential donors in this early phase is essential. After flying under the radar for several years and making the inevitable midcourse corrections, there is a much greater likelihood that a viable enterprise will emerge that can succeed in obtaining institutional status.

This approach has proven itself consistently. Most of the successful interdisciplinary efforts began this way, and the ones that didn't have reinvented themselves after the fact by shrinking and then reemerging based upon operational lessons learned. Bio-X, the renowned multidisciplinary center at Stanford, began as a simple collaboration between two young professors, one in biochemistry and the other in physics. It then expanded to their respective labs and then to biology and the schools of engineering and medicine. All of this took place on an ad hoc basis. By the time the signature Clark Center was constructed, scores of faculty from all over campus were collaborating around an effort to reinvent medicine. Similar stories underlie the creation of the Beckman Institute at Illinois, the School of Engineering and Applied Sciences at Harvard, the Institute for the Arts and Humanities at UNC, and literally hundreds of others. The challenge is to resist the attraction of mega-grants or donations as well as the notoriety of launching something big at the outset. Too often such efforts, in the words of one professor, lose steam and eventually become at best unnecessary overhead and at worst an embarrassment and ultimately a problem for those who championed their existence.

At Duke University, the concept of looking carefully before you leap has even been institutionalized. The vice provost for interdisciplinary studies heads a process designed to answer fundamental questions about scholarship, educational mission, and the practicalities of space, resources, faculty, staff, and sustainability. The primary focus is how a proposed center would allow the university "to accomplish something different or better than what can be done within existing departments."[4] An application process requires a plan, a budget, and by-laws, and if the center does proceed it is with the understanding that its mandate is for a five-year period, at the end of which it will be carefully reviewed. Duke refers to this as their "sunsetting process." Establishing as a matter of policy that centers do not necessarily exist forever removes a major impediment to innovation and entrepreneurial thinking in academia. The mistakes that inevitably occur when something new is undertaken do not have to be permanent ones.

Leadership Is Critical

The creation of successful multidisciplinary centers is almost always about individuals. Of course committees, administrators, and processes are part of doing something new in a research university, but we learned over and over again that the mission and culture were most often set by a far-sighted, inspirational, patient, and entrepreneurial leader. The story of Ruel Tyson, a professor of religion at the University of North Carolina, and his efforts to create the Institute for the Arts and Humanities at UNC illustrates our point. Beginning in 1968, Tyson had full enrollments for his iconoclastic, multidisciplinary courses with titles such as "The Banquet" and "The Morality of Knowledge." Ultimately he concluded that the conversations he was having with his students and other members of his department needed to be expanded to include colleagues throughout the arts and humanities. He started with a series of brownbag lunches and learned that the same opportunity for exploration that was so attractive to his students resonated with colleagues he did not even know. The brownbag lunches turned into seminars and then into a "program." A small ramshackle building called West House, with a tiny galley kitchen and an outdoor patio of sorts, was given over to the effort; soon the brownbag lunches became semester-long faculty seminars allowing six to ten professors full-time leave from their normal teaching and administrative duties in order to pursue their scholarship and, equally important, engage in a free-wheeling conversation with Tyson and a group of their peers from across the university.

Tyson understood that, under the guise of leading a faculty seminar, he was identifying the most promising members in the College of Arts and Sciences, and the seminar experience had a dramatic impact on faculty retention. In fact, for the first decade, none of the faculty Tyson brought into the program left the university. Realizing he needed to reimburse departments for the semester-long sabbaticals that were at the heart of his enterprise, he took his seminar on the road to engage potential donors who, he thought, might also be intrigued by the conversation that was taking place in West House. Tyson became a magnet for some of the university's biggest donors, and they jammed living rooms in New York, Atlanta, and Charlotte to get a dose of Tyson and his "conversation." Many attendees were former students, and they eventually formed an advisory board that, with the help of an industrious development officer, began turning Tyson's connections into substantial contributions. The fledgling enterprise became an institute; the faculty seminar morphed into a faculty fellowship program, and in 2000 ground was broken on Hyde Hall, the new home of the IAH. To date, Tyson and his successors have raised more than $49 million on behalf of the IAH, and more than 450 faculty members drawn from throughout the university have participated in its programs. Even Dean Smith, the legendary UNC basketball coach, joined a faculty seminar in connection with the writing of one of his books, *The Carolina Way*.

Tyson's efforts illustrate all we think is important about founding and leading interdisciplinary centers. He was originally an unlikely leader who was more interested in teaching and challenging students than in departmental or university innovation. From the very beginning of his academic career, he was interested in "reconnecting the dots" by thinking creatively about subjects that did not fit into traditional disciplines. His big idea, the faculty seminar, grew out of those ad hoc brownbag lunches. Once he understood its impact, he stuck to it tenaciously and recycled it continuously as he built the Institute for the Arts and Humanities. For Tyson, relationships were always at the heart of his work. When he first needed help building his enterprise, he turned to former students for seed funding while at the same time using the seminar to develop enthusiasm and support among faculty for this effort. The same approach worked with larger donors for whom being part of Tyson's conversation had evolved into an important part of their lives. Toward the end of Tyson's career, his admirers often characterized him as an academic entrepreneur. At the beginning of his quest, he likely wouldn't have known what the term meant.

The Conversation Is the Most Important Thing

For years, Jim Spudich, a distinguished biochemist at Stanford, and his colleagues had been planning Bio-X, a center that would build on their interdisciplinary work in bioscience and begin to transform human health. One day, Stanford's president, John Hennessy, called with some bad news. The Bio-X building would cost more than planned, and something would have to go. The plan was to eliminate the eating area in the basement of the Norman Foster–designed building. Spudich didn't hesitate in his response. "John," he said, "cancel the laboratories and build the cafeteria."

Spudich was right. Something remarkable takes place at lunchtime every day at the heart of the Stanford campus. Blue-jeaned chemists stream out of a building called Beckman, and lab-coated doctors start walking out of the medical school. Professors and students from engineering, biology, and physics join them. The age range is twenty to seventy; the demographic could only be described as multicultural, and, in some cases, young children accompany their parents. They are all descending on a 240-seat cafeteria called Nexus located in the basement of the Clark Center, home of Bio-X. Long lines form at multiple food stations. The lines move quickly, and then fan out into a vast, window-filled room supplemented by an outdoor terrace with tables shaded by brightly colored umbrellas. Long tables accommodate large and small groups, and a set of couches and coffee tables provide room for more intimate dialogue or solitary reading or computer work. A walk around the room at 12:30 P.M. evidences an extraordinary set of conversations. Chemists talking to doctors. Math geeks with laptops pointing at simulated models of virtual lungs. Engineers and physicists looking at pictures of medical devices. The room is full and people are waiting for empty tables. It stays that way until mid-afternoon and also draws a crowd for breakfast and dinner. In between meals, Peet's Coffee on the third floor serves coffee and tea along with muffins, brownies, and other snacks. The baristas seem to know almost every customer by name, and the intimate indoor seating and outdoor tables provide still another venue for dialogue.

It is not clear which comes first, the interdisciplinary conversation or the venue that encourages it. We suspect there is a multiplier effect. However the causation shakes out, the experiences at the Nexus cafeteria and Peet's Coffee powerfully validate Jim Spudich's admonition to John Hennessy to "cancel the labs and build the cafeteria." This is the same theme that anchors Ruel Tyson's vision for the IAH. It also began with conversations over lunch and grew into a place that facilitated dialogue among different disciplines. To this day, the magnificent fellows room in Hyde Hall, home of its multidisciplinary seminars, along with a huge kitchen where up to ten people can gather for lunch or coffee, foster the kind of new thinking that emerges from the nexus of various perspectives.

Fundamentally, a conversation is at the heart of any interdisciplinary project, and if such dialogue does not exist in the first place, the chance that it will be fostered by a new center or institute, even with a setting like Nexus, is remote. Once launched, the quality of the interaction that accompanies an interdisciplinary effort is the best measure of its success. More formal metrics such as grants received, faculty attracted and retained, and research undertaken and published are necessary and will vary depending on the mission. But anyone attempting to assess the work of a multidisciplinary effort should spend some time listening to the conversations that are going on. Hearing world-class academicians truly talking to each other across disciplinary boundaries is a sign that important work is taking place.

Pay Attention to the Space

At UNC, the process of creating a space for the IAH began in West House, a white bungalow on the campus with a conference room that seated no more than eight comfortably. Fourteen of Ruel Tyson's advisors were jammed around the conference table. Miraculously, the institute had just been granted permission to construct a new building on the main campus. There was agreement that the central location and the unique mission of the IAH demanded an extraordinary building that embodied its core values. At this point a wise advisor remarked that an extraordinary building requires a great architect, and that requires a great client. The process had begun. Every detail, from the exterior brick, to the equipment in the huge eat-in kitchen, to the interior of the Fellows Room, where fellows meet to share and consult with each other, was considered carefully. The degree of client involvement, according to the architect, was much more like a residential than a commercial project—not surprising since Hyde Hall would be the new home to the institute.

The end of the story is as you might expect. Hyde Hall is nestled among adjacent buildings more than one hundred years old but at first glance looks like an old building itself. The circular Fellows Room, attached to the angular main building, is clearly the product of a late twentieth-century aesthetic. The seamless relationship between indoor and outdoor meeting spaces would never have appeared within the formality of eighteenth-century design. The "incubator" with its flexible floor plan and the kitchen with its upholstered banquet and high-tech equipment are not only innovative in design but reflect the rich and complex nature of the conversations that are at the heart of the IAH. The conversations gave rise to the building, and the building enhances the conversations.

The IAH experience is by no means unique. Our conversation with Jim Spudich, the founder of Bio-X, began not with a discussion of the convergence of multiple disciplines into a new form of science or the latest medical device to come out of the program's efforts, but with a description of his visit to London to see the offices of Norman Foster, the renowned architect who designed the Clark Center, the remarkable building that houses Bio-X. Spudich immediately loved the fact that Foster had no walls in his office. When he began to study Foster's work he concluded that it represents a reinvention of architecture just as Bio-X proposed to reinvent bioscience and transform human health. The Clark Center would be the home of Bio-X, and Spudich took that charge seriously, poring over construction drawings for a four-story, three-pod building that would serve as a hub between science, engineering, and medicine. The objective, according to Spudich, was clear: to embody and house the remarkable collaboration that was already going on at Stanford and, as a result, to make the collaboration all the stronger.

Not all interdisciplinary projects can have physical spaces like the Clark Center or Hyde Hall. Both the Bio-X and IAH had strong lives prior to the construction of these remarkable buildings. In the early days both were housed in makeshift surroundings that, in retrospect, only add charm to the stories of their ultimate development. However, if the interdisciplinary conversation is powerful enough it will give rise to an appropriate space, and when that time comes it is critical to pay attention to everything about that space as a means of adding energy to the conversation.

A Case Study: Bio-X

Predictably, Bio-X began with a problem that Jim Spudich couldn't solve on his own. In late 1980, he was trying to understand how molecular motors work and was employing research from the emerging field of neurophysics. He had hit a dead end; in his own words, his "back was against the wall."[5] He discovered a paper by Steven Chu, a physicist he admired, about laser traps that could capture micron-sized particles; they were a promising avenue for Spudich's stymied research. The other good news was that, unknown to Spudich, Chu had recently moved to Stanford, and his lab was located nearby. After only a few conversations, a collaboration began. Spudich sent scientists from his lab to work with Chu, and together they built a trap that could be employed in Spudich's research. Chu sent four or five of his students to Spudich's lab to learn about DNA. The collaboration led to a wildly successful approach called single-molecule analysis, which spread rapidly around the world among scientists attempting to understand life's most fundamental building blocks.

One day Chu called Spudich with a grand idea. It was time to break down the barriers between all the departments that were interested in some form of biology, a number that was growing rapidly not only because of the breakthroughs that seemed possible in understanding the chemistry and physics of cellular and genetic material but also because it was becoming clear that living organisms had much to teach about other important scientific problems. They dubbed their project

"Bio-X," meaning "bio-everything." Much to their surprise, the name one colleague thought was better suited for a B movie caught on and sticks to this day. So, in addition to their own collaboration and their own distinguished science (Chu subsequently won a Nobel Prize for his work in physics and is now the U.S. secretary of energy), Spudich and Chu began to build something bigger, though they had no idea what that might be. They did know that when you maximize interaction among smart Ph.D.s and postdocs from a variety of scientific fields to focus on a common problem, sparks fly.

But great science takes more than sparks, and the reality associated with funding soon set in. The original research they were proposing did not synch up with priorities of conventional funding sources, and science is expensive. A cross-disciplinary thirteen-person committee was formed. The group had expanded to include faculty from engineering, medicine, and biology. Spudich was named the first director for a three-year term. It soon became clear that a hub was needed to facilitate all of the collaboration that was taking place in the intellectual space carved out by Bio-X, but it was important that this new hub supplement and enhance the departments themselves. Significantly, the founders themselves made clear from the outset that they would not be leaving, physically or intellectually, their own departments or disciplines. In one meeting it was established that this would only work if all the overhead dollars and all the glory went back to the departments. This principle was one with which Stanford's president, John Hennessy, strongly agreed, and a funding strategy was developed that focused on the construction of a building situated at the intersection of virtually all of the disciplines associated with Bio-X. Programmatic funding from the president's office would eliminate the need for Bio-X to operate from overhead generated from research grants. With help from the Internet boom, funding for the building was secured from Jim Clark, the founder of Netscape, and others. Hennessy committed $10 million from funds controlled by the president to provide initial funding for programs. Bio-X was off and running.

What took place next was an extraordinary vetting process. The idea was to identify people who truly wanted to collaborate and not, in Spudich's words, "Nobel laureates who were threatening to leave."[6] In 1999 a multidisciplinary panel awarded a series of core grants of $150,000 each with an eye toward projects that mimicked the collaborative spirit represented by Spudich and Chu. The idea was that this seed capital would provide enough "juice" to get collaboration started, and if there was merit in the work it ultimately would be self-sustaining. Another round of funding took place in 2002 when twenty-one projects were funded, and those two rounds of funding resulted in research that brought $70 million in new funding to the university. In 2006, the third round of funding generated 108 letters of intent from 222 faculty members and 54 proposals from which 24 were chosen.[7] At the same time, needed infrastructure such as sophisticated x-ray equipment, electron microscopy, and micro-arrays were spread out all over campus in an effort to insure that Bio-X was not merely a physical location, but a true cross-campus collaboration.

The results to date speak for themselves. More than 350 faculty members from 60 departments have participated on Bio-X teams tackling research problems in the life sciences and biotechnology. The mission has grown in breadth and in focus to include imaging and simulating life, restoring the health of cells and tissues, decoding the genetics of disease, and designing medical devices and molecular machines. The research itself has become even more multidisciplinary. Bio-X emphasizes what it calls a synthetic approach that attempts to go beyond the understanding of individual cells and molecules to an understanding of how proteins assemble into molecular machines—how muscle cells work together to make a heart beat or neural cells generate complex behaviors. All of this activity attracted Dr. Carla Shatz, a neurobiologist from Harvard, to assume leadership at Bio-X as its fourth director, and she plans to build on the extraordinary interdisciplinary tradition that in her words "exists throughout the Stanford culture. Here it is not just top-down. There is also a commitment among the faculty to solve important problems without regard to departmental boundaries."[8] Shatz thinks the key to Bio-X's success is its willingness to support innovative research. She is determined to build upon the original grant program, now called the Bio-X Interdisciplinary Initiatives Program, with a new plan called Bio-X Ventures which will commit $1 million or more to larger scale efforts aimed at the truly big problems in the field. She picked the term "ventures" because she does not believe the commercial sector should have a monopoly on the word. In her view, audacious research that attempts to connect the dots in a different way is a high-risk venture that offers high rewards. She believes that if places such as Stanford are to meet their responsibilities to the world such research ventures will play a central role, and interdisciplinary centers will almost always be at the heart of the effort.

Cooperation among the disciplines is critical to solving big problems, and this reality will inevitably impact almost every aspect of the entrepreneurial research university. But for every successful interdisciplinary initiative, there will be scores of failures, and even initiatives that do succeed will probably experience some near-death moments. Everything we have learned about interdisciplinarity suggests an entrepreneurial approach will increase the likelihood of success. Dispense with grandiose beginnings and start small. Build upon actual academic conversation and real cooperation. Look for an entrepreneurial leader who can assemble the required financial and human resources, withstand the false starts, as well as fashion and articulate a mission. Devote as little time as possible to academic politics and structural issues on the front end and resolve them once real problem solving can be demonstrated. Admittedly all of this will lead to a certain amount of chaos, but an entrepreneur would call it ferment and creativity, just the kind of activity a twenty-first-century research university must encourage if it is to be a true engine of innovation.

Leadership

As we've said, innovation begins with entrepreneurial thinking, and more often than not such thinking starts with an individual and not a committee or task force. For universities to become the engines of innovation we envision, a unique brand of leadership is required, and it starts at the top. Judith Rodin, who served as the president of the University of Pennsylvania for many years, put it best: "We need to role model . . . those attributes we want faculty to emulate and create a climate that allows entrepreneurship and innovation to flourish."[1]

In interviewing academic leaders who embrace an entrepreneurial leadership style, we discovered some key commonalities. First, an effective and entrepreneurial leader articulates the mission and values of the institution—a way of thinking about virtually every activity that takes place within the university community. Although typically broad and subject to interpretation, a well-crafted mission statement and a related set of values provide daily guidance to people all up and down the organizational chart. A stated mission is also inspiring. Going to work every day with the goal of addressing one of the world's big problems is the kind of motivation that can lead to extraordinary performance by individuals and teams. Most important, a leader dedicated to innovation understands that merely administering a set of rules within a rigid and hierarchical structure will not foster innovation or an entrepreneurial approach to problems and opportunities. She understands that a broad mission is empowering, providing creative people throughout the institution the encouragement and space they need to innovate. When this empowerment is coupled with the concepts of accountability and impact, it creates a high-performance culture that embraces change as a form of opportunity.

Of course, the specifics of mission and values will vary from campus to campus, and there is no one right way. The history of most research universities provides a starting point for articulating the core beliefs of the institution. Developing the "right" mission is less important than committing to having one that the university community understands and embraces. For this to happen, the leader must be comfortable with conversations about aspirations and enduring values. In interviews, public appearances, small conferences, and even one-on-one meetings, the leader can articulate the most fundamental principles of the institution and use them to shape decisions about immediate problems. Similar behavior will be adopted throughout the university, and a sense of mission and deeply held values will permeate the culture. A leader understands this and views such a result as a top priority.

Second, the leaders we interviewed clearly understood that their job is more about creating a culture than tinkering with a structure. They know there is no shortage in academia of people adept at making, interpreting, and enforcing rules. In any large institution there is an important role for the rule makers, and effective leaders understand and respect the function these people play in allowing the institution to function efficiently, consistently, and transparently. But an entrepreneurial culture thrives in a climate that celebrates creativity, innovation, and excellence. An effective leader builds such a culture at every opportunity, more often than not with small but symbolic actions.

At a regular biweekly meeting chaired by a newly appointed dean of the College of Arts and Sciences and attended by all of her senior lieutenants, one senior associate dean gave a long explanation about a set of rules that prohibited a particular course of action. The dean asked, "Well, who made these rules anyway?" After a long silence someone said, "Well, I guess we did." "Precisely," the dean replied, "and we can also change them." The story of this encounter has been retold countless times, most recently by the new dean of the same college in describing her approach to the job. She said she used to think the dean's job was to help people understand the rules and, where necessary, work around them. She now thinks the job is to evaluate the rules and, where appropriate, change them.

Strong leaders understand the viral effects of a story like this. Such stories help people understand that rules can be changed if necessary to achieve institutional priorities. Effective leaders see opportunities to impact university culture in virtually every action they take, from how they organize their office to how they conduct meetings— and especially in how they spend their time. If they stay at the job long enough, the culture will come to reflect their own personalities and views of the world. A leader with an informal style who has a habit of asking questions and enough humility to welcome advice will create a very different culture from that of a leader with a formal personality. Good leaders are clear both about their role in creating a culture and about the culture they seek to create.

Third, our interviewees spoke about the importance of strategy in providing a road map for the day-to-day activities of a large institution. While mission, values, and even culture must transcend the events of the day, strategy identifies a set of activities that combine to make an institution different from its peers. The goal is to create a sustainable comparative advantage. Even skillful execution without a well-crafted strategy will lead to confusion and ultimately a continuation of the status quo. But effective leaders develop a strategy first and then employ it throughout the institution to make important decisions. Judith Rodin told us that "being highly strategic is one of the most important qualities of a university president."[2] Although the process of developing a strategy typically involves many members of the community, initiating the process and ultimately articulating the result is the job of a great leader.

Fourth, the leaders we talked to understand and actually enjoy execution—the day-to-day process of translating ideas into reality. Erskine Bowles, former chief of staff to President Clinton and current president of the University of North Carolina System, described his approach to preparing himself for the job: "I did a ton of homework. I read everything I possibly could about the University. . . . I studied the history. I studied the long-range plan. I studied the budget of the system . . . and of each individual campus."[3] He went on to describe a process of assuming office that involved the creation of clear goals within the context of the university's mission and a method that he described as "execute, execute, execute" within established timelines and with clear accountability for all concerned. In fact, in all of our interviews with university leaders, we saw in them a willingness to roll up their sleeves and master the intricacies of matters they deemed important.

Of course, there is a big difference between effective management and micromanagement. Good leaders are team builders and delegators. They don't attempt to do their colleagues' jobs. When it comes to their own responsibilities, however, they attack them passionately, and they master the intricacies of specific tasks both as a means of getting things done and as a way to model behavior. At the University of Pennsylvania, President Rodin took on the enormous challenge of redeveloping West Philadelphia as a way of showing students, faculty, and alumni that a university could not talk of impacting the world's biggest problems while ignoring difficulties in its own backyard. It is much easier to demand of others a mastery of the facts and thorough preparation if you exhibit a willingness to do the same.

In a large institution, execution is impossible without the help of a skilled team. Erskine Bowles put it this way: "If there are a hundred reasons why an organization is successful, you can make numbers 1–98 a strong, proven, effective management team."[4] Effective leaders have been team builders all their lives, and this fact reveals itself early in the conversation. They give credit to others and minimize their own contributions. They spend an extraordinary amount of time interviewing new deans and personally checking references because, as one president told us, "I can find out things no one else can." They value a diversity of opinion and shun an approach that relies heavily on a small group of hand-picked, likeminded advisors. Another university leader we interviewed brought with him to his new job a tight-knit group of extraordinarily bright but inexperienced lieutenants, none of whom had a previous connection to the institution he had been called upon to lead. The result was a tumultuous relationship with the faculty and state government and ultimately a retreat to the status quo he had hoped to change. Effective leaders typically have a history of building outstanding teams whose members have deep and diverse experience, a track record of solving complex and nuanced problems, and a willingness to challenge the new leaders' assumptions.

Fifth, the leaders we spoke to actually like raising money, which is important because it is their job to lead the university's development efforts. They like raising money in part because they are typically competitive, and raising money is a means of "keeping score." More important, one president spoke of engaging with donors over critical university issues because donors often have a perspective and a point of view different from those of his academic colleagues. For him, engagement was not an artifice designed to make a donor feel important; rather, it stemmed from a genuine desire to learn something new. The process results in a virtuous circle. The leader broadens his circle of advisors and confidants to include important donors because he genuinely values their advice and counsel. The donors feel more connected to the institution because its leader has seriously engaged them in matters of importance to the institution. As donors become more connected, their level of commitment to the university goes up, and so does their giving.

Not surprisingly, the leaders we are describing here and the donors we talk about in a later chapter have a great deal in common. They both take an entrepreneurial approach to problem solving. They are results oriented. They like to beta test initiatives before they make a long-term commitment. They believe in measuring impact as well as institutional and individual accountability. Ultimately, donors invest not merely in an institution but also in an individual. The leaders we interviewed are adept at putting a human face on the development effort.

Personal style, as we've already said, is critical. Effective university leaders are as comfortable in the student cafeteria as in the state legislature or the boardroom. They are as likely to have lunch with the parents of new students as with a foundation president, and they know the names and family histories of groundskeepers as well as university trustees. If anything, they overcommunicate, never missing an opportunity to deliver their core message. The best are described by their colleagues as "being everywhere." To paraphrase Woody Allen, they understand that a huge part of their job is showing up, and they build enormous good will by doing so.

They are also good listeners. Erskine Bowles described his first visit to the each of the sixteen campuses he manages as one where he "listened, really listened . . . [for] about twelve hours at each campus."[5] Another president describes his dinner with a high-profile philanthropist as one where he simply listened, and by the end of the evening he had won the philanthropist over.

Managing crisis and uncertainty is always a huge challenge for any leader, but the leaders we talked to were likely to see opportunities where others see problems. The current financial problems facing all major universities provide an example. John Hennessy, president of Stanford, told us the decisions he had to make when running a high-technology business prepared him well to think about the steps required to respond to cutbacks in available operating funds and a reduction in endowment at Stanford. It is not that such decisions are welcome, but good leaders view this kind of challenge as an opportunity to make their universities run more efficiently. Such leaders also adopt a level of disarming transparency in the face of difficult challenges. On our own campus, we provided regular video reports on the progress of a survey by management consultants Bain and Company to reduce administrative costs and improve operating efficiencies. Although this work engendered a good deal of concern everywhere on campus, periodic updates throughout the process reduced the anxieties that come with uncertainty.

The chairman of one search committee thought personal attributes were so important that after a list of the desired qualities in a candidate had been compiled, he had it printed up on a wallet-sized card and laminated so each committee member could carry it with him or her until the process was complete. While the duties of a university president are to some extent negotiable, and their relative importance may differ from institution to institution, the specific personal qualities required are fundamental.

Our list of personal qualities begins with people skills because at least two-thirds of the job for a university president involves recruiting, assessing, motivating, and inspiring people. Strong leaders quickly determine what it takes to succeed in a particular job and whether or not a particular individual is a good fit. They have high standards and are confident enough in their own ability to surround themselves with team members who have complementary skills and are willing to disagree. Their sensitivity to the needs and motivations of others makes them great recruiters and inspires extraordinary loyalty. One associate in a technology transfer office at a large research university remarked that her entire outlook changed when a new president was named because she knew she could call him if she ever needed to and he would understand her problem. She thought she probably wouldn't need to talk to him more than once a year, if that often, but if she did, she knew she could.

An effective leader has an exceptional ability to connect with people, and to give all a sense that they have important personal and professional relationships with the person in the corner office. Effective leaders understand it is these individual connections, often made during brief encounters on a one-by-one basis, that provide the foundation for virtually everything they seek to accomplish. As Drew Gilpin Faust, president of Harvard, puts it: "An enormous amount of my job is listening to people, trying to understand where they are, how they see the world so that I can understand how to mobilize their understanding of themselves in service of the institutional priorities."[6]

This isn't to say that such a leader is not willing to make tough personnel decisions. To the contrary, being tuned in to personal dynamics provides the insight and confidence to act decisively, especially when an individual is impeding the effectiveness of a team or group. Strong leaders understand and embrace the fact that their job is primarily about people, and the skills required have been on display for their entire careers. These are not skills we all possess, but they are mandatory for leaders who seek to provide bold leadership at a research university that is striving to be an engine of innovation.

The leaders we spoke to are also hands on. They are willing to dive into the details of matters that are important to them even when the result is likely to be unpleasant. They let the team do the fun stuff, while they take on the chores no one else wants to do but that are truly important to achieving the shared goals.

Increasingly, the most important issues facing research universities are complex and nuanced and cannot be resolved at 50,000 feet. Instead, resolution requires fact-based analysis and consideration of the implications across multiple dimensions. Mastering the details results in a better decision and one that can be persuasively articulated. Innovative leaders understand the issues at hand because they do their homework and more often than not are among the best informed in the room. Like their comfort with people issues, attention to detail is typically not an acquired trait but rather a habit of the mind, an essential way of thinking, among leaders of innovative universities. Their discussion of important issues builds on specific examples, and they are comfortable with the numbers, frequently using statistical analysis to make a point. Rather than assume that others can worry about the details and that their job is to think big thoughts, they believe that the best ideas are developed from the bottom up and are built upon a deep understanding of the problem to be solved as well as the implications of all possible solutions.

Being hands-on should not be confused with taking on the jobs of others. In our interviews with effective university presidents we often heard the phrase, "that is why you have a provost." Effective leaders rely on their chief operating officer (referred to in academia as the provost), their chief development officer, and their key deans for effective execution of the operations of the university, and they empower these people to make decisions without the fear of being second-guessed. Both publicly and privately they are as likely to defer a question to one of their colleagues as to give a detailed answer. Ultimately, these leaders engage in a delicate balancing act—delving deeply into the relatively small number of issues for which they have responsibility and deferring the remainder to others.

At the end of virtually every meeting, and once a decision has been made, an effective leader asks the same question: How do we communicate this? Telling the story in an accessible and transparent manner is a huge part of their job, and our leaders employ many methods to get the job done. Many write handwritten notes which appear on the desks and sometimes even the walls of their key constituents. An increasing number of these leaders have their own blogs and employ video messages as often as memorandums to communicate with the broad university community. They cultivate media relationships and never miss an opportunity to involve the mass media as a means of advancing their agenda. Although these leaders are not always great public speakers, they are uniformly great communicators because they understand and utilize all of the tools at their disposal. In their view, the handwritten note sent to the right person at the right time can have a more significant impact than a university day address that took weeks to perfect.

The best leaders of innovative universities are decisive. They preside over structured meetings with predetermined agendas and timeframes, and at the end a decision is reached and responsibility for implementation is assigned. They don't revisit a decision once it is made, and they don't put off making a decision once the facts have been assembled. This decisiveness is often viewed as a breath of fresh air in an environment known for endless study, committees on top of committees, and a desire to put off until tomorrow even decisions that call out for resolution. Such leaders do not confuse decisiveness with impulsiveness. They collect the facts before making a decision. They understand that decisiveness can have a dramatic impact on the academic culture and can help unlock the entrepreneurial mindset we advocate.

The personal attributes we have described so far could arguably apply to a leader in almost any environment. The leaders we have in mind are uniquely qualified to lead a research university because of their deep commitment to the ideals embodied by an academic community. In most cases, their professional training took place in academia, and their mentors are mostly academics. Many expect to return to academia when they relinquish their leadership position. In their view, the university is home, and this reverence for the institution is also part of their being. Their impatience, constantly pushing for improvement and looking for opportunities to innovate, is a sign of respect for an institution they care passionately about and therefore want to improve.

A Profile of Effective Leadership

Listing a set of duties and personality traits is a start, but to truly understand what is required to be a true leader of a university, it helps to meet one. John Hennessy, the president of Stanford University, made his academic mark in the area of computer architecture and design, where he has published extensively and coauthored two well-known textbooks. His career at Stanford included service as chair of the Department of Computer Science, dean of the School of Engineering, and provost before he assumed the role of president in 2000. He was the first Stanford president trained as an engineer.

While deeply committed to academia, Hennessy was simultaneously engaged as an entrepreneur. In 1981, he assembled a team to focus on a form of computer architecture known as RISC (Reduced Instruction Set Computer), and the success of these initial efforts led him to use his sabbatical year in 1984 to found MIPS Computer Systems, a venture-backed company based in Silicon Valley now known as MIPS Technologies, a leader in the design of high-performance microprocessors. He has been a formal and informal advisor to Stanford students who founded such companies as Yahoo and Google. Hennessy has served on the boards of Google and Cisco Systems, among other companies.

To understand John Hennessy and what makes him tick we need only to spend an hour with him and then listen to a few of his talks. We met John in the lobby of the Fairmont Hotel in Washington, D.C., where he was attending a meeting of the American Association of Universities. We began talking about the economic meltdown, and he immediately launched into a discussion about the mistakes he made at MIPS. At the same time he mused that despite the difficult times faced by Stanford and other research universities, they were no more challenging than those faced by a start-up company, and he was sure he would be having a much more difficult time in the current environment if he hadn't been through that experience. In the first five minutes of our encounter, Hennessy had talked about making mistakes, the challenges currently facing academia, and the lessons of a high-tech start-up.

When we asked him about the impact of being an entrepreneur on his current role as president of Stanford, he remarked: "When I started MIPS I didn't know anything about business. I didn't have a clue. In general, engineers don't know anything about business. Build it and they will come."[7] But John soon came around to his strengths: "Being able to make decisions, especially financial decisions, in the face of uncertainty is clearly a skill I learned from my involvement with a start-up. In a start-up you can't wait or it will be too late. This is the case now with universities. Those that wait too long to respond to our current economic environment will be at a significant disadvantage." He also suggested that experience as an entrepreneur was helpful in raising money for Stanford: "Business experience is helpful when talking to the modern donor. Such donors are looking for a social return for future generations. They are interested in outcomes and long-term impact. It is critical to be able to speak their language and relate to them in [such] a way that they feel their philanthropy will make a difference."[8] In a lecture at the Stanford School of Engineering he summed up his views with the following: "Starting a company and talking to customers taught me to be a better teacher and a better author. If I could explain something to a customer I could explain it to a student or a reader."[9]

Hennessy also commented on Stanford's mission. He told us that Stanford decided to make its goal to attack the world's biggest problems because the university "perceived a huge vacuum. Bell Labs and PARC were closing and the private sector alone was not going to be adequate to go after these problems. The problems were increasingly complex and demanded an interdisciplinary approach. The university had many of the resources required. It seemed like a big opportunity that was worth going after."[10] In his lecture at the Stanford Engineering School he went even further: "If universities don't work on the world's biggest problems, who will?" He hastened to add that academic silos will not yield the kind of results he expects, saying, "You can't go after these problems if you are fixed in concrete. University structure must be flexible and the focus must be on the problems themselves, not the existing departments."[11]

Hennessy also eloquently makes the case for the importance of entrepreneurial thinking in encouraging innovation within universities: "Entrepreneurial leadership challenges [face all of our important institutions, including] startups, the Ciscos and Intels of the world, and universities. The question is how do you nurture and grow innovation." His answer: "Entrepreneurial thinking that understands innovation is the key." And at Stanford, he said, "the heart and soul [of the university] . . . is its entrepreneurial way of thinking." He went on to explain, "We need to learn how to apply entrepreneurial thinking to completely different contexts. For example, we created a course called Entrepreneurial Design for Extreme Affordability and out of it have come such ideas as a solar lantern for rural India and low-cost baby incubators."[12]

Finding the Right Leader

The hardest thing about finding an entrepreneurial leader is deciding if you really want one. There are several reasons for deciding against such a course. It may result in rapid change to an institution that traditionally moves slowly. It will inject entrepreneurial thinking into the dialogue of the university community. It will encourage participation in that dialogue by many who have previously been excluded. It will result in some highly visible failures. It will expose the search committee or decision maker to criticism for not taking a more conventional route. If the decision is made nevertheless to move forward, the following suggestions should be helpful.

We begin with the ultimate decision maker, the person or committee that will make the final choice. Everyone involved should understand exactly what kind of leader is being sought, and, ideally, every step in the process will reinforce that intention. Gaining such alignment is best accomplished not by some public pronouncement or interview in the press but rather through a set of subtle actions that might include developing a list of ideal personal characteristics, informal conversations with other university leaders, assembling the names of potential candidates, and, most important, considering the size and composition of the search committee. All of these actions culminate in the instructions to the search committee. If the instructions are clear and precise there is a higher likelihood the committee will recommend one or more acceptable candidates.

Picking the right search committee is essential to hiring the right leader. It is helpful if some members of the committee come from outside the university and have an entrepreneurial frame of reference — an openness to nonhierarchical leadership, a commitment to innovation, and a willingness to take a chance on a candidate who does not neatly fit all of the traditional criteria. It is also important that the committee be as demographically diverse as possible, because this will result in better decision making. It is often said that it is virtually impossible to find one person who embodies all of the characteristics of a great academic leader, but it is possible to appoint a committee whose combined membership does embody those qualities. Picking such a committee will dramatically increase the odds of locating and recruiting a great candidate.

The ultimate decision maker, through his charge to the search committee and the search committee itself, should drive the process. A headhunter can be a useful part of the process. However, the headhunter works for the committee, not the other way around. Headhunters can assemble a list of potential candidates, but the best candidates might not even apply without encouragement from committee members or the decision maker. Headhunters are also great at developing job descriptions. Effective search committees take their instructions seriously and actively engage with the headhunter in crafting a job description that accurately describes the candidate they are seeking. Headhunters may also seek to lower the expectations of a search committee in a legitimate attempt to inject realism into the process. The entrepreneurial members of the committee will be unpersuaded. They are accustomed to pursuing the unattainable. They are also great recruiters, and once they have a candidate in their sights, they are unlikely to let that person get away.

Another critical element of the hiring process is the final interview. Typically the committee recommends more than one candidate, and it is after they have all been interviewed by the decision maker that a final choice is made. These final interviews are typically long, personal, and comprehensive. In one instance we know of, they took place off campus in an informal setting; each lasted several hours and included a meal. The interviewer had exhaustive staff work at his disposal, and he used it to address every issue that had been identified and how it impacted the carefully crafted list of qualities the ideal candidate ought to possess. Even after this exhaustive interview, at least one candidate was called back to explore a set of follow-up questions. Assuming there are up to three final candidates, these exhaustive final interviews involve a major time commitment from the decision maker and from the staff that supports the process. We cannot think of time better spent. If the decision maker is willing to make the level of commitment we suggest, roll up his or her sleeves, and get deeply involved in the details of a final decision, the benefits of a wise choice will manifest themselves for years or even decades to come.

7

Academic Roles

In a nation in which many work into their late sixties and a newly minted Ph.D. is usually close to thirty, academics can expect a forty-year career. Traditionally, they know what to expect from the outset: a career of research and teaching, publishing in academic journals and books, writing grant proposals, and presenting papers at academic gatherings. These activities are often supplemented by service on departmental and university-wide committees and other administrative duties. In a relatively few cases, an academic goes into administration because the challenges are appealing or the pay is better, but most return to the academic life when their term is up. For many, this career is satisfying, and it should be. What we call the traditional scholar is the foundation of the research university.

It is a commonplace in higher education to say that good research supports good teaching, and we believe this will continue to be the case. Changes in the classroom stemming from the technological revolution mean that professors can share their expertise with a greater number of undergraduates while mentoring a group of graduate students who support their teaching and research. In the language of an entrepreneurial university, this alone increases the impact of a scholar's work.

When scholars employ new technology to teach the basic principles and techniques of their disciplines, they have more time for matters that require direct engagement or small-group discussion. With assistance from graduate students, professors can take advantage of new styles of measurement to build into their courses clear objectives, measurable goals, and specific time frames. While this might sound formulaic and even in some ways antithetical to the academic mission, such an approach can be liberating by providing a structure for meaningful interactions between mentors and students who can best learn the nuances of an academic discipline through personal interactions with a mentor.

The best of these scholars inform their own research agendas with the demands of their departments and disciplines and the needs of their graduate students and the university community at large. All departments need a cadre of faculty who research and publish prolifically and whose work is influential and cited by colleagues in their fields. This is how their peers judge the quality of a department, and those judgments have a direct impact on the ability to recruit graduate students and new faculty. Scholarly research is also important because it strengthens the core disciplines, which remain the building blocks of the university we envision. An emphasis on peer-reviewed research is also important for graduate students completing their doctorates and launching their careers. It is difficult to become a chemist or a historian or a philosopher without producing outstanding, peer-reviewed research. A distinguished university needs departments that are well respected and attract top graduate students and faculty.

For scholars willing to embrace an entrepreneurial mindset, however, the options are greater. We define below several of these options, including the public scholar, the translational scholar, the artistic scholar, and the engaged scholar.

The Public Scholar

Virtually everything public scholars do is aimed at a broad audience. Instead of writing a syllabus they write a textbook, and their classes are often productions involving hundreds of students and multiple graduate assistants. Their research passes scholarly muster, but they also write for a wider public on topics drawn from their scholarly work, and occasionally their books become bestsellers. Their lectures may be commercially available on DVD, and they are regulars on the lecture circuit or become experts called on by mainstream media. This role is uncommon in any university because it takes a unique set of talents. Only a few academics have the skills required to connect with a mass audience, but if a measure of academic success is impact, the public scholar ranks highly.

Our colleague Bart Ehrman is just such a public scholar. A professor of religion, Ehrman learned early in his career that writing a textbook was a good way to supplement his income. When his first attempt was a success, he went on the lecture circuit. His interactions with the public convinced him to write a popular book based on his research, and he has published a stream of books for wider audiences. Titles such as *Misquoting Jesus: The Story Behind Who Changed the Bible and Why* and *Jesus, Interrupted: Revealing the Hidden Contradictions in the Bible (And Why We Don't Know About Them)* grew out of Ehrman's research. *Jesus, Interrupted* made the *New York Times* bestseller list, and in the spring of 2009 Ehrman appeared on the *Colbert Report*—an unusual venue for any religious scholar.

The Translational Scholar

The role of the translational scholar is typically embraced by scientists or engineers working at the intersection between basic research and commercialization. Translational scholars balance complex relationships with the private sector and government—both of which provide important support for their work. The profiles provided earlier of Bob Langer and Joe DeSimone give a picture of this approach. The role of translational scholar has appeal for others in the academic community as well, especially as funding sources now demand multidisciplinary approaches to the world's biggest problems. In the medical school, translational medicine involves doctors, natural and social scientists, and public health professors and practitioners in efforts to formulate country- or region-wide approaches to such conditions as obesity and diabetes. Economists and other social scientists are increasingly integrated into problem-based scientific teams in order to provide evaluation mechanisms and recommendations for implementation. Engineering schools and schools of applied science partner with business schools to optimize problem-based research. All of those involved can be characterized as translational scholars. Without question, the role of translational scholars is challenging, but the opportunity for dramatic impact on difficult and important problems is extraordinary. Translational scholars have a major role to play as research universities evolve into engines of innovation.

The Artistic Scholar

Artists have traditionally played an important role in the university. Musicians, actors, dancers, writers, and filmmakers are welcomed as part of the faculty even without advanced degrees. Artistic achievement has been deemed a sufficient credential for admission to the faculty and even for the awarding of prestigious named professorships. A faculty appointment allows artists to continue their work while imparting their craft to eager students anxious to learn from a practitioner. The role of artistic scholar is well established and important, though not necessarily innovative in the sense that we are using it.

That could change, however. The radical change taking place in almost all contemporary art forms will inevitably expand and transform the role of the artistic scholar. The economic models underlying music, literature, and filmmaking are in flux, making each ripe for innovation, and academia offers an ideal setting for exploring new models. The same environment that gave rise to the Internet and social networking is ideal for fashioning responses to forces that threaten the viability of traditional record labels, publishing houses, and movie studios. Similarly, the growing importance of video as a means of communication will inevitably impact what is taught in universities. The convergence of artistic forms and the increasing use of technology create opportunities for collaboration between graphic artists, computer scientists, and performance artists. In addition, artists are searching for mechanisms for becoming more self-sustaining and are beginning to adapt lessons learned from social entrepreneurship to their projects and enterprises.

If rapid change is the most fertile ground for entrepreneurial thinking, then artistic scholars have an unprecedented opportunity to engage with the university in addressing the fundamental problems confronting the artistic community. Like the other problems we have described, they will require interdisciplinary approaches as well as participation from individuals inside and outside the academy. Artistic scholars who begin to address these problems will carve out important and viable long-term roles in the academic enterprise.

The Entrepreneurial Scholar

Earlier we introduced two academic entrepreneurs, Jim Spudich and Ruel Tyson. Although they think of themselves as traditional academics, they have a penchant for entrepreneurial innovation. It was

Jim Spudich who suggested to Stanford president John Hennessy that if money needed to be saved during the construction of the Clark Center, Hennessy should cancel the laboratories and keep the cafeteria. And Tyson, who took his faculty conversations on the road, channeled his ability to facilitate provocative communication into an important and lasting institution.

By nature, academic entrepreneurs ask for forgiveness instead of permission and can often be a thorn in the side of administrators charged with running an efficient university. Entrepreneurial scholars are builders who understand the importance of symbolism whether it is in the design of a building or the mission statement of a project or institute. They search for resources inside and outside of the academy and enlist the help of people who have had no previous connection to academia. They facilitate dialogue by being inquisitive and are more interested in solving problems than placing them in well-defined compartments. These people are enablers. They supply a vision, assemble the necessary resources, and create an environment for those resources to thrive.

The Engaged Scholar

The number and influence of engaged scholars is growing rapidly as it becomes clear that students have an increasing interest in social change and universities are being called upon to address the major problems of the world. New and exciting career paths are emerging for those who choose to combine their academic pursuits with a commitment to a broadly defined view of service. Engaged scholars can take a number of career paths. They can develop service-learning courses and programs that combine academic rigor with experiential learning centered on a particular project. For example, a class at Duke University led by Dr. Emmanuel Katongole, a professor of theology and world Christianity, focused on a girls' school in Rwanda and combined on-site volunteer work with classroom study of the political, economic, and social realities of the region.

Most state research universities are involved in major initiatives aimed at improving the economic development of their state and region, and the demand for such initiatives is increasing. Faculty from diverse backgrounds can help initiate these programs and, more important, be called on to evaluate them. Social entrepreneurship programs, courses, and initiatives are burgeoning on most college campuses, and there is huge new demand for courses on topics such as microlending, environmental and health policy, green energy, and venture philanthropy. Important research, typically multidisciplinary, will inevitably grow out of these course offerings. Because the opportunities are so new, they are open to faculty in the arts and humanities and physical and social sciences, as well as those in the professional schools. On our campus, a professor of communications studies who also happens to be a distinguished filmmaker co-taught a course on artistic entrepreneurship with the campus executive director for the arts. Many of the students in the class secure internships in nonprofit arts organizations that are attempting to develop sustainable long-term business models. In the coming years, the number of our colleagues who choose to become engaged scholars will, we suspect, increase more rapidly than any other group.

Academics often lack the background or training necessary to embrace new or unconventional roles. Ultimately, success involves accepting a course of action that is often foreign to their academic experience. Here we offer a few thoughts on how academics might adapt to these new roles.

Don't Try for a Perfect Score

Many academics spend most of their lives being "the smartest kid in the class." For them, getting straight A's was expected, and taking tests was a sure way to shine. In graduate school they were encouraged to undertake work that was highly specialized in order to do something unique and original. If they achieved in programmed ways, they could expect to get tenure, the defining mark of an academic career. Fashioning a career in one of the roles we have described is fundamentally different. It is an iterative process with many midcourse corrections. Often the projects these roles demand fail—especially the first few times they are undertaken. Approaches must be adapted to fit the particular environment. What is important is to get started, knowing that the first attempts may be far from perfect. In fact, we can almost guarantee that if the project is executed exactly as it was originally envisioned, it will surely miss the mark.

Five Years Is Forever

The traditional university often assumes permanence in its plans and programs. The tenure track offers secure employment. Endowed programs imply a steady flow of funds without regard to the performance of the project. As a result, new programs face complex vetting procedures that make approval a long and arduous process—understandable when something is "forever." In the university we envision, academics must be prepared to trade the permanency of a fully endowed project for the impact that can be achieved by a more provisional endeavor. A five-year time horizon should be the standard for most initiatives, and in the early stages, this time horizon might be contracted to one or two years. The beta test, in which an idea is launched in a low-key way without much fanfare and improved in response to initial feedback, is likely to become the norm. The funds to support such efforts will typically need to be renewed annually, at least at the beginning. After multiple iterations, some level of permanency can be achieved for the very best projects, but permanence should not be the ultimate goal. Instead, solving big problems and maximizing impact should be the drivers, with the understanding that future funding will be conditioned on results achieved and the importance of the problem being attacked.

You Can't Do It by Yourself

In order to have maximum impact and successfully address complex issues, academics will almost always be engaged in a team effort involving participants from on and off campus. This is the antithesis of the independent-contractor model that typifies so many academic careers. Those who will ultimately be most successful in the roles described here will consult a diverse group at the very earliest stages of their various undertakings. Informal lunches and discussions in the homes of alumni will often precede groundbreaking initiatives. Building a team early in the process not only provides a basis for seed funding and administrative support but also makes the project better by introducing a wide variety of points of view.

The best thing we did when considering the creation of a course of undergraduate study in entrepreneurship was to host a dinner for a group of entrepreneurs. We steered the discussion toward the kinds of things entrepreneurs need to know before beginning any new enterprise. The conversation went on for hours, and the ideas expressed became seminal in our thinking about how to teach entrepreneurship. Five years later, many of the participants are strong financial supporters of the program, and others are now on the faculty.

A corollary to this fundamental principle of inclusion is that you can accomplish more by giving others the credit. In fact, the high-impact scholars we have described are constantly looking for opportunities to recognize others, express their gratitude, and develop opportunities for their colleagues to achieve their goals.

Commit to Metrics

This is the hardest part. Academics, even those whose professions are based upon precise measurements and standards, resist measures designed to evaluate the success of their programs or careers. Within a traditional university setting, the resistance is understandable. For instance, it is hard to measure the impact of a liberal arts education, and the appropriate time frame for evaluation is not a year or even five, but more likely an entire lifetime. Similar issues exist within traditional departments, institutes, and programs, largely because what constitutes success is often unclear and subject to debate. Academics whose focus is on important problems accept the necessity of measurable goals and actionable metrics. In fact, they demand these metrics as a means of benchmarking success and a valuable instrument to attract further funding. Accountability is valued because it focuses the team, energizes potential donors, and helps justify the extension of the short time horizons discussed earlier.

Learn the Skills Required

Simply describing a set of career choices is not enough to support a cadre of academics who wish to embrace new roles for themselves and undertake high-impact projects and initiatives. With this in mind, we created at UNC a four-day annual entrepreneurship boot camp that takes place right after commencement. With the help of department heads, deans, and others, approximately twenty faculty members are identified who have an innovative project or initiative in mind and seem to be comfortable with modifying or changing their approach to their careers. The curriculum includes the most important elements from UNC's courses in entrepreneurship, both traditional reading and case studies, discussions with faculty who have mounted successful projects, meetings with commercial and social entrepreneurs, and work on an ongoing, university-based project that is entered into a competition on the last day. Areas of study include opportunity identification, strategy, marketing, execution, and finance—subjects we believe are as important to academics as they are to entrepreneurs. The curriculum is fully immersive, with late afternoons and sometimes evenings devoted to team-based projects initiated by the participants. The teams present their work to a panel of judges on the last day. The judges include university administrators, alumni, and local entrepreneurs, all of whom can provide support to the projects being presented. By the end of the sessions, participants have at least some of the basic tools required to undertake a major project or even to re-imagine their academic careers. Measures of success are the number of projects started and whether they reach sustainability, as well as the success of the participants in advancing their own career goals.

Culture and Structure

Inside academia, it's hard to talk about the university's impact on the world's great problems without getting immersed in a conversation about faculty rewards and university structure. Discussions about enterprise creation or entrepreneurship in the university can quickly become debates over whether faculty should be rewarded with promotions and tenure for securing patents and creating businesses. Discussions of institutional innovation and how to attack big problems often bring up questions about how the university ought to be organized, whether the new program ought to report to a dean or the provost, or if the leader should be a center director or a department chair.

The time spent on these discussions, of course, is time not spent on solving critical problems. Actually addressing global warming is more important than determining who gets credit for it or whether to create a new unit to house the project. Creating the right culture and the right team with the expertise, resources, and passion to tackle a problem will have greater impact than arguing about developmental structures or the overhead allocation for a particular grant or contribution. In the abstract, academics usually agree that addressing critical problems is more important than debating organizational issues, but putting that belief into practice is sometimes difficult.

In this chapter, we discuss the difficulties involved in achieving consensus in universities. The passion and vigor that characterize debates over organizational issues grow out of a sense of the importance of the institution and a sincere belief that the way it is organized affects how it carries out its mission. So while we might suggest that preparing to take on the great problems of the day could be done more efficiently with less debate over the fine details, we nevertheless value the love that faculty have for their disciplines and the passion they feel for their institutions.

Silos and Where They Come From

Universities are criticized, fairly, for being obsessed with organizational issues. Stories about the viciousness of academic infighting are legion, but we contend that turf protection and silo-driven thinking are no worse in universities than they are in other large institutions. Pharmaceutical companies produce drugs with toxicity problems because the division that discovers the drug is focused on potency and does not talk to the division that certifies safety. Investment banks separate wealth management from risk management, resulting in a process where more risk is taken with the client's money than with the assets of the bank. The disconnects resulting from silo-driven thinking are very much the same from enterprise to enterprise. The solution is to develop an outwardly focused perspective and constantly to ask the questions, precisely what problems are we trying to solve, and how do we do that better?

The silo mentality is legendary in higher education. Students in one school want to take classes in another school at the same university and cannot cross-register. Logical places for academic buildings are ruled out because housing or athletics has their eye on the same spot. And most important, the great problems requiring input from multiple disciplines are neglected because two deans or two development officers cannot agree on matters of control and credit.

So why is this silo mentality endemic to universities and, in fact, most large institutions? Roger Martin, dean of the Rotman School of Management at the University of Toronto, suggests an answer in his book *The Responsibility Virus*. He believes that a cycle of over- and under-responsibility gives rise to a compartmentalized organizational structure designed merely to perpetuate itself, as opposed to a culture that adapts itself to attack the problems it was created to solve. In this cycle, a leader becomes aware of problems in a particular unit, takes too much responsibility, and starts solving the problems alone. This process marginalizes the unit manager, leading to his dismissal and recruitment of a new manager. The leader has great confidence in this new manager and takes that particular unit off the list of problem units, but of course none of the underlying problems that contributed to the poor performance of the previous manager have been addressed. When the problems resurface, the cycle repeats itself.

The underlying causes of the responsibility cycle have to do with intrusive leadership that opts for shuffling managers instead of addressing real problems. The cycle breeds managers more concerned about the well-being of their individual unit than the customer or task the unit was created to address.

Examples of this "responsibility virus" in universities are everywhere. The dean of a school will not collaborate on fundraising because he does not want to fall behind on his own campaign goal or lead the unit that has to lay off development officers. Faculty members want to withdraw from their department and form a new administrative unit because they feel the public service they perform or the interdisciplinary nature of their research is unappreciated by their colleagues. Deans do not enroll students in interdisciplinary programs because they cannot figure out how to share the tuition dollars among departments. These behaviors continue to take up an extraordinary amount of time, energy, and intellectual focus while the great problems universities should be addressing remain unsolved. Martin, himself a university administrator, acknowledged to us that the responsibility virus is endemic to universities, but he also believes that the extraordinary longevity of universities partially offsets the slow pace of change, creating the opportunity to produce transformations that will have impact over literally hundreds of years.

What Doesn't Work

Silo-driven thinking that impedes the making of important decisions permeates research universities and is inconsistent with solving big problems. Both of these points must be addressed when creating the university we envision. Before we suggest potential solutions, we want to discuss some approaches that will become increasingly difficult to implement and that seldom work.

CREATING PERMANENT INTERDISCIPLINARY STRUCTURES

An entrepreneurial faculty member has decided to address global warming. To do so, she needs to bring together colleagues—chemists, biologists, and physicists—who have the technical expertise to produce new energy sources. She also needs the participation of those who have the ability to understand environmental impacts: marine scientists, climate specialists, and computer modelers. People who understand the policy implications—political scientists, policy studies faculty, sociologists, and even philosophers—are also needed. Rather than simply assemble the team, this entrepreneurial faculty member goes to the provost and proposes the creation of a new School of Climate Change. The provost protests that the administrative costs of the program will be high because a new dean, new development staff, and lab and office space are required. Department chairs oppose the idea, asserting that they will lose valuable colleagues and the academic luster that accompanies them. The dean of arts and sciences and his development officer are worried that new gifts to support the study of climate change will not count in their arts and sciences fundraising totals or provide administrative fees. The dean also worries that students will begin to leave the college for the new school, taking their tuition dollars with them. The president doesn't want to create yet another silo.

But our enterprising young faculty member is not deterred. She gets a big oil company to provide a $50 million gift, creating the new School of Climate Change. The provost relents because there's now enough money to fund the new project. The president agrees because a high-visibility project has been funded on his watch, and the central development staff gets to count the big gift in its overall campaign total. The dean of arts and sciences agrees to be a team player. The School of Climate Change is formed. A high-profile dean for the new school is recruited to great fanfare, but the appointment triggers the need for more administrative infrastructure than the big gift provides. Years later, the $2.5 million in yearly expendable funds has generated a new vice provost and scores of new nonacademic employees, while the earth is still getting warmer.

REORGANIZING EXISTING UNITS

A new president comes to a university. In her initial listening tour she hears of growing frustration from all sides. She hears from students that higher education is outdated. Students are interested in solving the world's great problems but fail to see a correlation between the academic disciplines and their social concerns. As a result, many of the best students spend huge amounts of time and energy on causes they believe in at the expense of the classroom experience. Similarly, they often spend summers doing volunteer work as part of commercial overseas programs rather than participating in the university's study abroad offerings because the academic component seems irrelevant.

Other members of the university community are also frustrated. The alumni hire recent graduates and conclude they cannot write, and for some reason the recent hires have not taken Introduction to Shakespeare, which alumni thought everyone "had to take." In this view, the great problems of society are the result of the erosion of traditional academic values, and the recent slippage in the *U.S. News* rankings would certainly be solved if everyone took Shakespeare. The faculty also expresses frustration. Humanists believe it is obvious that theory is where the action is; social scientists are stampeding to quantitative models; and the scientists are harshly divided between those who want to work on multidisciplinary problems and those who want to protect "the core."

The conversation escalates to the board of trustees. The president makes a bold announcement that she is appointing a blue-ribbon panel to study the future of higher education and examine the current organization of the university. There is much infighting and politicking over who is to serve on the panel. After a year, the panel produces a list of recommendations that involve the reorganization of the university into new units such as life sciences, humanistic theory, environment, and quantitative behavior. The new plan is implemented amid high-level fanfare, but the faculty and chairs in the traditional disciplines never buy into it because the changes do not reflect any fundamental change in the way teaching and research are undertaken. At the first hint of an economic downturn requiring university budget cuts, the traditionalists assert their point of view under the auspices of fiscal discipline, and the old organization again predominates.

CHANGING THE "REWARDS SYSTEM"

Discussions about the university's becoming more problem focused almost always end in a debate about how tenure and promotions are awarded. These debates come in two varieties. The first is over the language of the tenure regulations. In these debates, proponents argue for the explicit inclusion of some or all of the following as grounds for awarding tenure: technology creation in the form of patents or licenses, formation of start-up businesses, public and community service, creation of works of art, and advancement of the public understanding of science or research. These outcomes are all desired by various stakeholders, so proponents claim that if we "count" these things toward tenure or promotion, we will build a system that will produce these outcomes. The problem is that changing the wording of the regulations has almost no impact on those who vote on a candidate. The granting of tenure is a subjective process, and the voters are tenured academics who are highly invested in the tradition that allowed them to achieve academic excellence. The faculty will take care to consider the regulations however they read, but ultimately neither their vote nor the tenure process in general will be changed by the addition of new criteria to a set of regulations. We strongly support a broader interpretation of faculty roles in universities, but we don't think simply changing regulations will produce the desired result.

The second debate relates to the first but is more fundamental; it concerns the criteria that should take precedence when making tenure and promotion decisions. This debate most often occurs when research productivity is pitted against great teaching, and research almost always wins. If the regulations are changed you can substitute company formation or social impact for teaching but the discussion remains the same, and, generally speaking, research will continue to win.

So how should these other important criteria get injected into the tenure discussion? One approach is to redefine what "counts" for research productivity in certain schools and include patents issued, companies founded, and public service, including impact on big problems, as part of the definition of tenurable scholarship. Jim Plummer, the dean of the engineering school at Stanford, says impact on big problems should be at least one criterion by which faculty research is measured, and Stanford engineering is not alone in this position.[1] Schools of engineering and applied sciences have considered this criterion in evaluating research productivity for years, and there is no reason why the concept of impact cannot be introduced in other disciplines to evaluate scholarly research. A comprehensive solution involves abandoning the zero-sum view for a broader definition of tenurable scholarship. If the culture in which tenure decisions are made is one that values scholarship that affects the world's biggest problems, criteria and processes will naturally evolve to reward research that ventures outside the purview of traditional scholarship.

The Fundamentals of a Different Approach: Culture Not Structure

We have explained why the conventional responses to the silo mentality are fundamentally flawed. They all rely on externally imposed solutions such as new organizational structures or regulations, and the environment itself emphasizes collective over personal responsibility. The alternative is for universities to develop a culture that values problem solving over organizational self-interest and encourages personal responsibility by empowering and rewarding individual faculty and students. Changing the boxes on the organizational chart will not produce a university that is an engine of innovation. What follows are some suggestions that focus on the cultural change that will create such an institution.

CULTURAL CHANGE TAKES TIME

First, it is important to recognize that cultural change will not come without sustained effort from academic leadership. Presidents and provosts cannot put "make the university more problem focused" or "break down the silos" on their to-do lists and then hope to cross it off after the completion of a short-term initiative. Universities become more problem focused only with a sustained commitment and with broad buy-in from leaders throughout the campus. It does not happen overnight, but when it does, the results can be dramatic. In the ten interviews we did on the Stanford campus, the conversation invariably began with the statement that Stanford's mission was to address the world's biggest problems, a message that is consistently heard from the president's office. Equally important, virtually all of the collaborative programs we learned of at Stanford received early moral and financial support from the president's office. In short, with a consistent message over a significant period of time and strategic encouragement, cultural change can take place even in an institution as complex and diverse as a research university.

BEWARE OF THE QUICK FIX

Making leadership appointments almost always generates enthusiasm and optimism in organizations. Just as there is no quick way to address systemic challenges, it is unlikely that a single person has the ability to solve what university leaders have struggled with for 500 years. A president committed to a problem-solving culture needs help from the deans of the various schools, and those deans must be committed to the mission and have a mindset that values collaboration. Putting such people in place and retaining them is easier said than done. The CEO of an integrated bank told us he identifies future leaders for his business by assigning people to projects that require collaboration between operating divisions. If they succeed at producing solutions, they are candidates for advancement in the organization. Similarly, President Faust of Harvard asked Professor Michael Porter to run a session at a dean's retreat that focused on the competitive advantage that "being part of Harvard University" gave to each member of the university. The idea was to build a collaborative mindset based on mutual self-interest. In making leadership appointments, universities must put more emphasis on this institutional mentality. Avoiding the quick-fix syndrome can best be accomplished by assembling search committees that embrace the kind of responsibility culture we discussed earlier.

University presidents cannot wait until a search committee has done its work and recommended two or three candidates before getting involved in the process. By then it is too late, especially when, as is often the case, one candidate has impressed the committee and become the only viable alternative. If a search committee is carefully chosen to reflect the values to which the institution aspires (this often involves including members who value inclusion and differing viewpoints and, where appropriate, knowledgeable and experienced alumni), it is more likely that its recommendations will include individuals who embrace the desired culture.

USE TASK FORCES SPARINGLY

Task forces are often a way to deflect pressure on a particular issue, but as a means of seeking community-wide consensus they are a great temptation for university leaders. When a difficult problem arises, it is easy to name a panel to examine it and produce recommendations. This provides a respite for six months or a year while the task force does its work, but the recommendations can be difficult or impossible to implement because those making the recommendations are not responsible for implementation. The end result is often another report that goes on the shelf with little follow-through. Meanwhile, months or years have elapsed while important problems remain unsolved. Task forces, while useful in building consensus or in sharing information, are unlikely to resolve difficult problems quickly or launch bold initiatives. The successful task forces are those that provide ideas and input but do not deflect responsibility from the institution.

FOCUS ON THE MISSION, NOT EXTERNAL RANKINGS

Universities will be ranked as long as producing lists sells magazines and draws readers to websites. In some ways, these rankings drive performance and, in the absence of other external measures, provide a way for trustees and system presidents to measure productivity. When the rankings are high they generate extraordinarily favorable publicity for the university. For all of these reasons, external rankings cannot be ignored. Unfortunately, performance driven by external rankings can produce unintended consequences inconsistent with the institutional mission and conducive to a silo mentality. At our university, we would be at the top of a ranking that measures Rhodes scholarships won, women's soccer championships, and the scholarly productivity of the Sociology Department and the School of Public Health. Needless to say, we haven't found a ranking that is limited to these measures. And beyond that, most ranking formulas provide external measures that are unlikely to encourage a focus on the world's great challenges or even provide students the basic building blocks for living a productive life. Moreover, rankings can be easily manipulated, as evidenced by revelations that institutional programs have been put in place for the sole purpose of influencing the rankings.

The alternative to being driven by external rankings is to devise measures that are consistent with the university's mission and clearly measure the objectives of the institution. This allows the creation of a mindset that says, "Here's what we want to do," instead of, "Here's how we get ahead of Universities X, Y, and Z in the rankings." Considering three rather simple metrics will illustrate our point. The first is the total number of applications to undergraduate, graduate, and professional programs. If the number of applications is going up, then one could conclude that the institution's academic reputation is attractive and the fundamental culture is resonating with a relatively objective audience: prospective students and their parents. A second useful measure is the amount of funding for research grants. While this measure has the attendant problem of valuing some disciplines, such as the sciences, that naturally attract large amounts of external funding over others, such as English, that draw far fewer grant dollars, those differences are well appreciated by university leaders and trustees and can be considered in devising a measure. Finally, gift income relative to a national average or selected peer institutions is a reasonable indicator of the buy-in of a key constituency to the direction of the university and the culture that has been created. Some would argue that these measures give too much influence to the market and may not be appropriate for some institutions, but the tradeoff is that these measures or others like them allow a university to set its own agenda rather than respond to externally created criteria that may not align with the mission of the institution.

Today, the average tenure for university presidents and chancellors is seven years.[2] The average tenure for deans and provosts is much shorter. At our university, we have had six deans of arts and sciences in the last seven years. Turnover at the dean and provost levels is common at universities that have integrated liberal arts colleges: of the sixty-two largest research universities, thirty have integrated liberal arts colleges, and only five of those have deans that, as we write this, have served for more than three years.[3] The turnover doesn't occur because of some systemic problem. It occurs for two reasons. First, being dean of a liberal arts college is good preparation for being a chancellor or provost, and therefore these deans are the first to be called when an opening occurs at home or elsewhere. At our own institution, our last three permanent deans of arts and sciences all became provost or chancellor, and three of our last four provosts now lead major research universities. Second, there are more universities than there are potential administrators who have mastered the tasks necessary to run them. Understanding this unmet need for academic leadership experience is vital to fashioning a strategy for stability.

Universities that have stable presidencies generally prosper. Steve Sample of the University of Southern California, John Casteen of the University of Virginia, and Mary Sue Coleman at the University of Michigan have all provided extended leadership to their universities and have outperformed their peers at other research universities by some measure. President Sample launched the second-most-successful fundraising campaign in the history of American higher education in USC's $3 billion effort and transformed the campus along multiple dimensions as a result.[4] President Coleman has made the University of Michigan one of the leading institutions for study abroad in the United States and has entered her university into the $100 million Michigan Innovation and Entrepreneurship Initiative. John Casteen, the longest-serving president at a top fifty school, has preserved UVA's esteem among educators despite heavy budget cuts from the Virginia legislature.[5] He accomplished this by decreasing the university's dependence on state funds, a controversial strategy that was executed adroitly. Stabilizing the president's position produces clear leadership and support for those on the leadership team, resulting in less turnover among deans, department heads, and other key administrators. Continuity in these positions breaks the cycle of task force reports and listening tours that inevitably accompanies new appointments.

We know from firsthand experience that achieving continuity is easier said than done. Not only are able administrators in great demand, but search committees guided by sophisticated headhunters often compete for the same individuals who meet criteria that are fashionable at the moment. The cycle can be broken by adopting a clear-eyed view of the administrative job market, again recognizing that there are lots of universities needing administrators. The best way to stabilize academic leadership is to identify candidates who understand the fact that from their first days as a dean they will get dozens of emails from search consultants saying that they are just the right person to go to another university and be a provost. It is therefore unrealistic to expect a long-term commitment from all key administrators. For provosts and deans, five years may be the most that can be expected; to get someone effective to stay longer is truly a special opportunity for a university. Henry Rosovsky's long tenure as dean of arts and sciences at Harvard is an example.

Fundamentally, our recommendations are twofold. First, hire individuals who understand the realities of academic leadership and the associated job market. Second, set realistic expectations for the tenure of key academic leadership and adjust accordingly. Able leaders will respond by infusing a bias for continuity throughout the institution and will ultimately recruit a senior team with both tangible objectives that will result in leadership continuity. Of course, continuity alone does not allow a university to achieve its potential, but it provides a platform upon which a culture of innovation can be built.

ENCOURAGE TEMPORARY COMBINATIONS AS AN ALTERNATIVE TO PERMANENT STRUCTURES

If culture is more important than structure in realizing the university we envision, then it should be easy to assemble problem-based, multidisciplinary teams to attack issues without encumbering the institution with a major long-term commitment every time such a team comes together. If administrative support, funding, and recognition can be achieved without creating something new and permanent or reorganizing some already existing department or school, energy can be directed to problem solving and away from turf protection. Problem-oriented teams could have five years to demonstrate their utility and could generally be funded with expendable, one-time resources during that initial period. The assumption should be that most of such groupings will maximize their utility during that period and will sunset at the end of their initial period of inception. This is what happens to most start-up enterprises. A very few will survive the first five years and become candidates for more permanent status based upon the achievement of clearly articulated, measurable goals. In this second phase, which might reasonably be expected to span five years as well, the initiative would attempt to reach sustainability through whatever means made sense. Of course, this second phase will, in all probability, look very different from the first, but what exists will have stood the test of time and have a much higher likelihood of long-term success. For example, seed funding for Bio-X at Stanford was completely accomplished with one-time money. When we asked John Hennessy what would happen if Bio-X failed, he said, "Well, I would have a very nice building that I could do something else with."[6]

It is certainly easier for academic leaders to make a commitment to a project that is battle tested and has proven its viability as opposed to one that is merely a glimmer in the eye of a promising young faculty member—even if it has been converted into a spectacular PowerPoint presentation. The major advantage of this temporary approach is that it places time, energy, and focus on solving problems and relegates organizational structure, task forces, rules, and regulations to the back of the room at least in the initial stages of a new enterprise. At some point, such matters must be addressed, but only when new ideas have become true ongoing concerns, increasing the likelihood that the energy that must be expended will have a high payoff.

We have described here a different outlook on the structure of research universities that is based on our belief that the challenges are more about culture and people than structure, rules, and regulations. University presidents, deans, and provosts hear good ideas every day. Turning the right ideas into reality and empowering the people who create them requires sustained leadership and management qualities such as compassion and empathy. At bottom it requires leadership that will stay the course with a commitment to creating a culture that places solving big problems ahead of organizational structure, rules, and regulations. This is the priority that should never come off the to-do list, even in the face of seemingly more pressing challenges.

Teaching Entrepreneurship

We are often met with skepticism, especially from entrepreneurs, when we tell people that we teach entrepreneurship in a university. Many entrepreneurs contend that "entrepreneurs are born and not made" and that entrepreneurship is not teachable. Our first response to this skepticism begins with the ideas of Peter Drucker. He was convinced that entrepreneurship is "not a personality trait," though people who need certainty are unlikely to be good entrepreneurs. Instead, Drucker asserts that entrepreneurship is based on concept and theory and can be taught. In fact, he believes the fundamental reason entrepreneurship is so risky is that "so few of the so-called entrepreneurs know what they are doing."[1]

Our second response to skeptics draws on a sports analogy. Dean Smith, the legendary basketball coach at UNC, could not instruct Michael Jordan in his dexterity or remarkable vertical leap—those are Jordan's God-given talents. In his three years with Jordan, Coach Smith was, however, able to impart the fundamentals of the game, instilling the oft-neglected principles of defense and footwork and transforming a talented recruit into one of the greatest players in history. Coach Smith could never have worked that magic on either of us. We don't have the basic talent to meet him halfway, but observing his work has taught us a great deal about basketball and about teaching.

We believe that a special set of attitudes, skills, and knowledge is required to think and act entrepreneurially, and we have seen hundreds of undergraduates, graduates, and faculty members over the years learn the entrepreneurial process and master the required entrepreneurial skills. We believe many of them will become successful entrepreneurs.

At the same time, each year we encounter students who conclude that becoming an entrepreneur is not for them. These students are often among the most talented, but they begin to doubt their future as entrepreneurs when they learn there is no "right answer" in entrepreneurship, and their doubts grow when they realize that no amount of preparation can guarantee success. Ultimately they decide a more structured career path will maximize their talents, although we expect that some will ultimately change their minds and give entrepreneurship a try. More likely, they will team up with an entrepreneur, providing a set of skills essential to a new product or enterprise.

Once academics and entrepreneurs accept the idea that the skills of entrepreneurship can be learned, a new set of objections often arise. Entrepreneurs usually contend that only an experienced practitioner, and not a cloistered academic, is qualified to impart the hard-won lessons of the seasoned entrepreneur. Faculty often object to the inclusion of entrepreneurship within the sheltered space of academia; entrepreneurship, they feel, belongs in business schools or somewhere that a trade is taught.

Academic training alone does not prepare someone to teach entrepreneurship, and academics typically lack the essential real-world experience so useful in teaching entrepreneurship effectively. Occasionally, academics happen to be entrepreneurs, but it is unrealistic to assume that academia will routinely produce instructors fully qualified to teach the subject. The answer, we believe, is to pair academics with experienced entrepreneurs in a manner that combines theory and practice. Achieving this partnership is admittedly easier said than done, and even when successful, the model involves a one-off, handmade approach that is extraordinarily resource intensive.

The trade-school critique advanced by our academic colleagues is based on a classical but outmoded understanding of entrepreneurship. Research universities are not the place to teach the skills of "replicative entrepreneurship," defined by Professor Will Baumol as the creation of any new enterprise ranging from a sole proprietorship to a nonprofit organization.[2] Teaching the intricacies of alternative legal and financial structures, government regulation, sales prospecting, and even the writing of a basic business plan is not particularly well addressed by the resources available at a university. Moreover, information vital to replicative entrepreneurship is readily available from a host of websites and other sources and can be communicated effectively outside the university. Teaching what Baumol calls "innovative entrepreneurship" is a different endeavor, however, and is precisely the kind of activity great universities should be engaged in.

The innovator strives to challenge conventional wisdom, synthesize information from disparate sources, communicate clearly, and keep an open mind when searching for answers. All of these skills are hallmarks of a liberal education. But apart from teaching the student how to think and communicate, the university also imparts the content of its core disciplines. Before creativity and synthesis can take place there must be mastery of an academic discipline. Entrepreneurship education can integrate with traditional university disciplines that teach students to think like chemists, anthropologists, or historians. That is why we argue strongly for a minor in entrepreneurship as a complement to a traditional undergraduate major in the liberal arts.

We begin this chapter with the premise that entrepreneurship is a way of thinking that can be taught using a carefully tailored and relatively expensive curriculum not easily expanded to large groups. We also believe entrepreneurship is a field of study that complements but does not replace traditional university disciplines.

We have been involved in teaching entrepreneurship to undergraduates in the arts and sciences for the past seven years. Close to 700 students have participated in the full set of courses required to receive a minor in entrepreneurship. Thousands have participated in one or more courses or other activities associated with our entrepreneurship curriculum. Based on this experience, we have reached the following conclusions.

Build a Foundation in the Arts and Sciences

Learning to think entrepreneurially can be extraordinarily valuable to students of law, medicine, engineering, or business, but, for a variety of reasons, we believe the place to start is with undergraduates in the arts and sciences. Beginning with the arts and sciences provides an opportunity to impact the core mission of the university because the humanities most closely reflect the values and culture of a liberal education. Moreover, the College of Arts and Sciences teaches the largest number of students. If students and faculty in what is often referred to as "the College" gain value from studying entrepreneurship, there is a high likelihood that the hearts and minds of the entire institution will follow. Even the very best entrepreneurship programs that begin in business or engineering schools risk being confined to those schools, potentially reducing any influence they might have had on the larger body of students and faculty.

We chose the Economics Department as a logical home for our curriculum, though there was some question within economics whether entrepreneurship was an appropriate area for departmental expansion. Subsequent events made the choice fortuitous. The American Economics Association established a working group on entrepreneurship education and an official category for academic research. The groundbreaking work of Will Baumol and Ned Phelps has given scholarly entrepreneurship increased credibility. In his 2006 speech accepting the Nobel Prize in Economic Sciences, Phelps referred to entrepreneurship several times, a first in such a setting. We also considered UNC's Chemistry Department for our entrepreneurial program, chiefly because of the extraordinary number of entrepreneurial projects the department has generated. Ultimately, identifying the correct department became less important than finding a committed champion (in our case the chair of the Economics Department) who was willing to sponsor the program and shepherd it through the administrative process.

Beginning with undergraduates in the arts and sciences also makes sense because they are often unfettered by well-defined career goals and are, for the most part, still considering multiple options while seeking their place in the world. Unlike contemporaries who have opted for career education in a professional school (undergraduate business majors, for example), arts and sciences students are less focused on their first job after graduation and more interested in exploration. As a group, they are extraordinarily bright, motivated, and idealistic. By their sheer numbers and their energy these students have a strong influence on the culture of a university. If a group of them gets excited about entrepreneurship, big and unanticipated things can occur.

Team Academics and Entrepreneurs

The "secret sauce" for teaching entrepreneurship is to team academics with entrepreneurs. This partnership is necessary for some obvious and not-so-obvious reasons. Clearly, those who teach entrepreneurship ought to think like entrepreneurs and have experience in applying the principles they teach. What is less obvious is how important an experienced academic is to the effort. An academic provides the intellectual content appropriate for what is typically a set of upper-level undergraduate courses and the teaching experience to impart it. Creating a curriculum that incorporates real-world applications is especially challenging. The presence of an academic also counters the perception that entrepreneurship is not a serious academic enterprise. This criticism almost always surfaces when entrepreneurship is taught solely by an entrepreneur, no matter how bright or committed to the academic enterprise he or she is. Lastly, an experienced faculty member is in a better position to handle the administrative responsibilities of any new academic undertaking, including course approvals and syllabus writing. Also, a personal interaction with a distinguished academic can correct misperceptions about universities that some outside entrepreneurs may have.

This team approach to teaching entrepreneurship has been demonstrated to work over many years. It was pioneered by Jeffrey Timmons, first at Harvard and subsequently at Babson College. For more than thirty years, Timmons and his colleagues have sponsored a one-week summer program, the Price-Babson Institute, designed to "teach how to teach" entrepreneurship. Every year, this popular seminar continues to draw attendees from around the world. The institute requires academics and entrepreneurs to attend in two-person teams in the hope that they will return to campus and work collaboratively. This collaboration works well in theory, but it can be difficult to identify the right team members. Entrepreneurs often fail to appreciate how hard it is to create a superior learning experience for students, and once engaged they are surprised at the huge time commitment required for teaching. For academics, the decision to join such a collaboration involves reconciling the time and energy they must dedicate to teach entrepreneurship with their career goals. The opportunities for publishing in entrepreneurship are limited, although that situation is improving. Support from colleagues and administrators may be minimal, especially from professors committed to a traditional view of their discipline or administrators bent on improving a department's rating. In identifying appropriate entrepreneurs to engage in team teaching, the task is to locate individuals with a track record of unquestioned professional success who have also remained connected to academia. An individual who is deeply involved with the university as a result of having teamed with an academic to launch an institute or finance a new facility is often a good candidate. Experience in academia gives the nonacademic an appreciation of the nuances and pace of the university and demonstrates partnership skills as well as commitment to the institution. We found an entrepreneur with a Ph.D. in chemistry to lead our efforts in scientific entrepreneurship.

On the academic side, the entrepreneurship faculty has been composed exclusively of senior, tenured professors with the freedom to undertake new projects. Identifying suitable faculty has not been as difficult as we initially expected. The opportunity to teach highly motivated, innovative undergraduates who want to make an impact in the world—and who aren't accustomed to taking no for an answer—has made the experience of teaching entrepreneurship highly rewarding for the professors, and as a result academic "superstars" have gravitated to the program.

Teach the Fundamentals

Entrepreneurship and entrepreneurs have become the darlings of the popular media, and interest in the field seems to spawn a new op-ed piece every week. At least one new entrepreneurship textbook appears yearly, and with the rise in the popularity of social entrepreneurship, the pace is picking up. In preparing for our course, we reviewed many of these works and learned something from each. Still, we fall back on a small number of classic works to provide the concept and theory that Drucker contends is essential. Fundamentally, we believe our job as teachers is to raise the right questions. To do this we focus on six areas: innovation, strategy, marketing, finance, execution, and ethics—and in each area we focus on one core idea.

Our definition of entrepreneurship begins with innovation and, not surprisingly, relies on Drucker's idea that innovation is not always revolutionary but often involves adjustments to an existing process or system that can be anticipated by understanding predictable demographic or cultural changes. The next big thing is more likely to be a rustling of the breeze than a huge explosion. Drucker's *Innovation and Entrepreneurship* eloquently states the principles of entrepreneurship—principles as relevant today as when Drucker first described them in 1993. Our students consistently report that Drucker's book and his conceptual framework comprise the most valuable theoretical approach offered in our curriculum.

We turn next to strategy because we believe this is where most entrepreneurs go wrong. They leap before they look and use a "ready, fire, aim!" approach. Entrepreneurs who ultimately succeed pause before they plunge forward—they aim to win the war before the first battle is fought. Our big idea in strategy comes from Michael Porter, the legendary Harvard Business School professor. In his words, "strategy is about being different," and for innovation to be truly sustainable it must embody a set of activities that result in a sustainable competitive advantage. Again, we use a classic text, Porter's "What is Strategy?" an eighteen-page article published in the *Harvard Business Review* in 1996. This basic manifesto provides a framework for turning opportunity into an actionable plan by outlining a set of critical questions: Is the opportunity or enterprise truly different? What are the activities required to sustain that difference? Most important, what activities must be eliminated or traded off to create lasting value?

When we refer to marketing, it is in the broadest strategic sense, beginning with the premise that no matter what the activity, there is always a customer (or more broadly speaking a stakeholder), and it is critical to determine who that customer is at the outset. The big, ongoing question here is, "What business or enterprise are you truly in?" Of course there is never a definitive answer, but continually asking the question focuses our students as they explore entrepreneurial opportunities. We use the work of the late Theodore Levitt to frame these questions. His insights from numerous articles and his seminal work *The Marketing Imagination* (1983) provide the basis for our inquiry.

Teaching the numbers presents the biggest challenge. Without question, any entrepreneur who is serious about creating a sustainable enterprise must understand how to model alternative financial scenarios, monitor the ongoing finances of an operating entity (especially cash), and obtain financial backing. Knowledge of accounting and finance is necessary, and giving students an elementary understanding of these subjects requires at least a semester. An accounting and finance course requirement might be the answer, but we have resisted establishing such a requirement (we do require introductory economics) because many of our most interesting and exciting students do not understand why knowledge of accounting is necessary to turn their ideas into reality, and such a requirement would discourage them from undertaking the minor. The epiphany that knowledge of finance is a good idea comes about halfway through their coursework in the minor, and many go back to take an accounting course.

Our current solution is to provide a lecture and an exercise designed to teach the fundamentals of an income statement. We teach another unit on alternative modes of finance. Our goal is to illustrate the importance of cash: How much will it take to start an enterprise, and where will it come from? How much will it take to sustain the enterprise? And how do you know how much is in the "shoe box" at any given time? Addressing these questions in class and with a review session before the final exam enables about half of a group of one hundred students to answer a relatively simple exam question covering the numbers; this is not an optimal result.

We continue to tinker with this part of the curriculum. We're experimenting with a six-hour module at the end of the curriculum that focuses exclusively on entrepreneurial finance. The question we will continue to ask is how does one provide the financial literacy entrepreneurship requires without losing many of the students who will most benefit from learning entrepreneurship and who will ultimately have the biggest impact upon society? We expect to generate and test a number of responses to this vexing problem.

We should add that the challenge of teaching financial literacy in an academic environment is not confined to teaching students. In fact, we happened to uncover strong interest in learning about the numbers among faculty and administrators when we offered a free three-hour session taught by the leading accounting professor on campus. The first course filled up in one day and was populated by academic deans, professors old and young, and administrative personnel of all ranks. The seminar has now become a regular offering by the business school. The most common motivation for attendance is to have some idea what the financial people are talking about or the desire to learn how to manage a department budget or a grant program. The interest in financial literacy in the university community at large is an important development, and we are paying close attention because it is clear that understanding the numbers is essential to creating an entrepreneurial university.

Execution is often overlooked in entrepreneurship—except among entrepreneurs themselves, the best of whom are relentless in their focus on the operational aspects of their enterprises. Whether Howard Shultz is worrying about the cleanliness of the bathrooms at his Starbucks stores or the late Dr. Govindappa Venkataswamy was concerned about the success rates for cataract operations at his Aravind Eye Hospitals in the poorest parts of India, successful entrepreneurs revel in the details of their enterprises. But how do you teach this attention to detail? For the most part it can't be taught in the classroom. We use Starbucks's success as an example of attention to detail and combine this case study with on-site observation to demonstrate the fastidiousness required to create the "Starbucks experience." We also expose students to monomaniacal entrepreneurs whose presence and style give students some sense of the single-minded focus required to make something new actually happen. There is no substitute for real-life experience in teaching what is required to actually implement an idea. Most of our students have come to the conclusion that no matter how good the idea and how clever the strategy and marketing plan, without relentless execution, new enterprises are likely to fail.

A section on ethics is a great opportunity to involve disciplines and departments that might otherwise not think of themselves as relevant to the education of entrepreneurs. We often start with the concept of social entrepreneurship. We stress the idea that doing well and doing good are not mutually exclusive. This idea has extraordinary currency among our students and is popular in other parts of the university community as well. We also introduce the concept of the "triple bottom line," stipulating that the success of any enterprise can be evaluated by its financial, environmental, and social impacts and positing techniques for measuring each.[3] Disciplines as varied as history, policy studies, environmental studies, engineering, chemistry, and political science can be consulted to develop concepts of impact. We also seek to pose and develop a specific ethical problem; we have used a film on Enron (called *The Smartest Guys in the Room*) and another about a start-up business (called *Startup.com*) to illustrate the slippery slope of ethical compromises and the inevitable ethical choices entrepreneurs will face as they function in a rapidly changing environment where rules are either evolving or nonexistent. We would prefer an independent course on entrepreneurial ethics that employs an interdisciplinary approach, but our curriculum is necessarily abridged. Our guess is that there would be no shortage of interest among academic departments in creating such a course, viewing it as an opportunity to round out the education of our budding entrepreneurs.

Employ a Variety of Techniques

Entrepreneurship is a contact sport and cannot be taught exclusively in the classroom using a traditional lecture method. In our teaching, we have settled on a mix of methods that combines highly interactive lectures in a large classroom setting (we have limited the size of this class to one hundred but in theory it could be much larger) with case-based discussion sections of no more than twenty-five students each, supplemented by outside speakers, specialized workshop courses, and internships.

Lectures are used sparingly and crafted carefully. In our curriculum, we employ lectures no more than once a week, replacing them with outside speakers about five times a semester. Our lectures are designed to provide an intellectual framework for each of the big ideas in the curriculum. Our approach is to engage students in a dialogue that draws upon contemporary examples of basic principles. For example, we use the creation of the iPod and of eBay to illustrate Drucker's approach to innovation. We cap that lecture with a video on the development of the container ship by Malcolm McLean to show how a small change in the way freight is transported has had a profound effect on the entire world. Even in lecture sessions, we encourage interaction in order to reinforce the idea that entrepreneurship is not a passive activity but a way of thinking; learning how to think like an entrepreneur requires engagement and practice.

We are committed to the case method as a teaching tool, and we use cases for roughly half the introductory course and throughout the remainder of the curriculum. Students read and brief a case study selected to illustrate a particular concept such as the importance of innovation to social entrepreneurs. The class is conducted in the Socratic method, using questions and answers to create a dialogue that reinforces basic principles introduced in the lecture. It is impossible to predict exactly where the discussion will go, and the instructor has to be willing to give up a good deal of control in exchange for spontaneity and excitement—not an easy task for many. Typically this is an approach that is new to both students and faculty and therefore requires special preparation by both. Students must be taught how to prepare a case (there are good cases that help teach this as well) and must be encouraged to come to class fully prepared and willing to actively participate. We base a portion of the final grade on some measure of class participation. For professors, we believe some form of instruction or systematic exposure to the case method is a necessity. Since the method is employed almost exclusively at law and business schools, faculty members trained in these disciplines have had extensive exposure to the technique. For untrained faculty, we suggest a multiday seminar such as the Price-Babson Institute at Babson College mentioned earlier, where the technique is applied specifically to entrepreneurship.

Guest speakers are either the best or worst part of the curriculum. The best speakers give students a sense that even the impossible is possible and that seemingly ordinary people can accomplish extraordinary things through focus and passion. The worst speakers are pedantic or ideological and seemingly incapable of self-reflection or admitting a mistake. Moreover, some of the very best entrepreneurs are simply boring. The very traits that make them great entrepreneurs make them poor public speakers.

Over the years, we have developed several techniques to maximize our chances of success with outside speakers, knowing full well that selection will always have some risks. First, it is important to spend time with the speaker in advance of the lecture or at least observe the person in a public situation. We suggest a lunch meeting and a class visit so the prospective speaker can get a feel for what is involved. Students are included in the lunch to see how the speaker interacts with a small group. At the end of the process we have a better idea of whether the prospective speaker will work.

Second, when dealing with high-profile speakers for whom pre-screening is not possible, we make sure a trusted colleague has heard them speak. When Ted Turner came to our class, we employed an interview format with the part of the interviewer played by one of Turner's colleagues, and the result was spectacular. We had an hour of candid, off-the-record conversation and a lively question-and-answer session that went far beyond his prepared speeches already available on any number of websites.

We also encourage speakers to interact with a small group of students at lunch before class. For students, this kind of interaction is often the highlight of the semester because of the opportunity to meet and talk informally with someone they admire. These meetings also give students the confidence to interact with people they might have once found intimidating. Students also learn that people, no matter how celebrated, love to give advice and do so willingly when asked. For speakers, these informal meetings are a great warm-up for the lecture, and the best speakers use the get-together as a learning experience, peppering students with questions about issues that are relevant to a current project or business. Often, speakers end up learning as much as they teach and volunteer to come back for a repeat performance.

We have also had success with inviting at least one speaker per semester who is closer to the students' age than we are. Young entrepreneurs seem to develop a unique rapport with students and impart a sense of what's possible. Despite the fact that some of these younger speakers left school to pursue their passions, none of our students has dropped out after hearing one of these young entrepreneurs speak. Increasingly, graduates of the entrepreneurship program who have turned their idea into a reality come back to fill the role of the younger speaker.

Workshops are the hands-on element of the curriculum. They usually revolve around the production of a detailed plan by a team of four or five students. In some cases we require that the plans be entered into a yearly campus-wide business plan competition, which tends to create a remarkable sense of focus and urgency among the teams participating. Each workshop focuses on a particular kind of entrepreneurship: commercial, social, scientific, or artistic, and we combine an academic and entrepreneur to teach each course. In the scientific workshop, we pair a chaired professor of chemistry who has entrepreneurial experience with an entrepreneur who has experienced extraordinary success in developing science-oriented businesses. In the arts, an award-winning filmmaker who teaches in the Department of Communications Studies is paired with an arts impresario or alternatively a professor of music is teamed with the founder of a record label. Outside experts get involved, generally in response to the needs of the student teams, to produce a viable and professional plan. Its presentation comprises the largest part of the student's final grade.

Internships are expensive, time consuming, wrought with operational difficulty, and essential to our approach. We are committed to providing hands-on experience. We have up to one hundred students a year undertaking some form of internship, primarily in the summer. Roughly twenty go to Beijing to work in emerging China-based enterprises usually run by English-speaking expatriates. The remaining students are evenly split between commercial and social or artistic enterprises. Interns are paid a stipend to offset living expenses if their host organization is unable to compensate them. Many domestic internships are secured by the students themselves, while others are arranged by a full-time internship director who manages all aspects of the program. Interns keep a diary or a blog (with the permission of their supervisors) and ultimately write a paper on their experience.

Provide Practical Tools

As we seek to provide students with both a theoretical basis for thinking about entrepreneurship and real-life experience in practicing it, we are constantly reminded that entrepreneurs require certain skills that can only be developed with practice. The first skill is encapsulated in what we call the "one-pager," which is exactly what you might suppose it to be. The idea is to explain your idea or conclusion in no more than one page because a fast-paced entrepreneurial world often allows the entrepreneur only one page to sell an idea. Moreover, the one-pager requires a clear understanding of the core concept being discussed, and the only way to learn this skill is to practice it. During the course of a semester we require numerous one-pagers on a variety of topics. We have been surprised by the difficulty students have at mastering this assignment. Students are much better at producing long, meandering proposals replete with digressions and footnotes than developing a focused, persuasive rationale in support of one central premise. If there is one measure of whether we have succeeded in teaching a student to think entrepreneurially, it is the one-pager. Those who master it are typically on their way.

Another set of critical skills involves presentation techniques, both visual and oral. The goal is for our students to be experienced enough to make a winning presentation to investors or supporters the first time out. In addition to learning how to write a plan, students learn and practice presentation techniques revolving around the production of effective and compelling slides—a practice that has become, for better or worse, a fundamental currency of entrepreneurship.

Once students understand the difference between merely transferring words to a slide and building effective visual images, the work they produce is typically superlative. Employing compelling images, full-motion video, and sound of all kinds, students produce presentations that make the PowerPoint presentations to which we have become accustomed seem shamefully outdated. Even those who have not yet learned to think like entrepreneurs can produce a visual presentation that will impress the most jaded venture capitalist or philanthropist. Students' oral presentation skills are not as well developed, but the only way to improve them is through practice. Before a student graduates, we try to create at least three opportunities for high-pressure verbal presentations that demand a substantial amount of preparation and practice. Pressure is generated either by the issuance of a grade (in some courses the final presentation of a project can account for the entire grade) or by participation in an outside competition in which winning projects receive support, the judges are well-known practitioners, and the public is invited to attend. These outside competitions invariably galvanize student teams and provide a degree of motivation far in excess of anything that takes place in a classroom. Results have been outstanding in classes that require participation in outside competitions. Students do well in the competition and work harder there than in any other class—they also report that they learn more from competition. The combination of a desire for recognition, the lure of cash prizes, and the fear of failing in a very public setting seems to be the key to learning presentation skills.

Limit the Size of the Undertaking

As should be evident by now, this endeavor involves a high degree of student-faculty interaction with an effective ratio of no more than 1:25 in introductory courses and approximately 1:12 in workshop sessions. The internship requirement is also labor intensive. We employ one resident internship director and a part-time director in Beijing to develop one hundred internships per year. As you might guess, this job is extraordinarily challenging because it involves not only finding internships and matching students with them but also troubleshooting all of the issues associated with thrusting undergraduates into the world outside of academia. Without question the 1:100 ratio for an internship program pushes the limit, and the quality of the program would suffer substantially if it were exceeded.

There is also the question of cost. Teaching entrepreneurship in the manner we suggest is expensive. Accounting fully for all costs, we estimate the minor in entrepreneurship costs $3,000 per student per year. By capping the number of students we accept in the two-year program at one hundred per year, it costs $600,000 per year, over and above normal educational costs, to run an effective entrepreneurship minor. Not all of these costs are typically reflected in the early days of such a program. Faculty and entrepreneurs often volunteer their time or provide it at a vastly reduced rate. Our estimates, however, provide a picture of the resources it will take to sustain a program over the long haul, assuming it is paying its own way and not taking advantage of the goodwill of participating departments and individuals.

Even if cost were not a consideration, attracting the necessary talent to develop a large-scale entrepreneurship program is a challenge. Recruiting leading academics and accomplished entrepreneurs to teach is no easy task. Even after a program becomes well established, a university that has not become truly entrepreneurial will retain innumerable barriers to accepting appropriate practitioners within its ranks. There are exceptions: Babson College has developed an entire institution dedicated to teaching entrepreneurship, and enrollment is in excess of 1,600 students.

Reach beyond Arts and Sciences

Although we firmly believe teaching undergraduates in the arts and sciences is the appropriate way to start teaching entrepreneurship, creating an entrepreneurial university ultimately requires teaching entrepreneurship throughout the community. The same basic approach we have outlined in this chapter can be employed to teach graduate students and faculty in the arts and sciences as well as students and faculty in the professional schools. We are experimenting with a graduate certificate that mirrors the undergraduate curriculum but with concentrations in scientific entrepreneurship and social entrepreneurship—the two areas of most interest. What is unclear is whether the demands of a graduate curriculum allow for a full certificate program or whether students would be better served with specialized courses that teach the basics in a series of modules, workshops, or even week- or month-long seminars like the summer program run by the business school at Stanford. All of these approaches are worthy of exploration.

Accountability

The call comes from the chairman of the board, the CEO of the company, or the biggest contributor to a project. The question is always the same: "How are we doing?" At times in our careers we had a simple response. We pulled up a "dashboard" or set of metrics that were updated daily or weekly and launched into an answer. "Revenues yesterday were $20,000 and averaged $17,000 over the last week. We have $500,000 in the bank and we should be generating cash in three months. We made a key new hire and the acquisition we have been working on fell through." A few questions about the details on each point would follow, and then we would hang up and go back to work. Of course, these conversations relate to our activities outside the halls of academia.

If a department chair, a dean, or a university president is asked, "How are we doing?" what often follows is a long pause and then a set of questions: "How are we doing with regard to what?" "Who are you referring to when you say *we*?" "What timeframe are you talking about?" Next comes a long conversation about the importance of priorities, the need for a strategy, and the pressure for clearly defined metrics that answer stakeholders' questions. Ultimately, both parties need a way to measure performance against a plan and provide focus for an agreed-upon set of activities.

To someone outside the university, this sounds like a straightforward and relatively simple task. In reality, it is extraordinarily difficult for the research university to foster the kind of entrepreneurial environment that accomplishes this seemingly straightforward goal. Constructing a president's dashboard for research universities—a dashboard informed by countless other dashboards throughout the institution—is the subject of this chapter and serves as a tool for answering that most crucial question, "How are we doing?"

We need this *über*dashboard and the smaller ones that power it because "how the university is doing" is no longer merely a private conversation between a friendly board chair, a donor, and a university president with an eye toward making incremental improvements. Now the conversation is a public one involving state legislatures, federal agencies, private foundations, the U.S Congress, and the general public, all of whom fund, directly or indirectly, the activities of a research university. Their questions have to do with enrollment (Who gets in?); affordability (How much does it cost and is it worth it?); stewardship (Are those growing endowments that accumulate tax free being employed responsibly?); and impact (Do research universities, the most elite institutions in our society, really matter?). These public conversations are increasingly played out in the media and other public forums and are often framed in terms of mandatory performance measures, reduced funding, or changes in the tax code that enact new requirements in order to maintain tax-exempt status.

The conversation is now taking place inside the walls of research universities as well. A dramatic reduction in endowment and outside funding in 2009 has caused research universities to examine every aspect of their institutions. Similarly, donors of all sizes want to understand the impact of their contributions. Students and their parents are interested in the return on their tuition dollars; board members view themselves as fiduciaries and want to insure they are meeting their responsibilities; and, as a result, faculty and administrators are examining virtually all institutional activities to determine whether they make sense. Increasingly the question is, "Do these activities fit with the strategic direction of the institution?"

So where do you start? It would be tempting to review the rankings, determine which are most relevant to your own institution, develop a set of initiatives that will favorably impact your own ranking, and then create metrics that track your progress.

Relying on rankings to measure the performance of a university, however, is a bad idea for a host of reasons. It cedes to an external body, such as the editors of a magazine intent on increasing circulation, the most important questions facing the institution. It precludes the development of a unique strategy consistent with the particular competencies, geography, history, and traditions of an individual institution. Most important, it forces the university into an execution trap where the only way to excel is to outperform its peers; this trap, more often than not, devolves into an arms race involving everything from the level of student aid to the quality of dormitories and athletic facilities. In the short run, continuous improvement initiatives can yield results that will be reflected in the rankings, but at some point they will produce diminishing returns. Ultimately, the only way to win this game is to continue to out-execute the competition, and that translates, more often than not, into a simple equation: whoever raises the most money wins.

There are variations on this formulaic approach that create equally bad results. Attempting to impress state legislatures or federal agencies by achieving high scores on externally mandated measures forces universities into the same kind of performance trap. Similarly, if the goal is to attract prospective students and their parents by building a new cafeteria or student center, the approach can divert resources from more important needs while providing a temporary competitive advantage, lasting only until peer institutions catch up. Relying solely on rankings to shape the dashboard by which a university is measured leads to a mentality and a culture antithetical to the engines of innovation universities can and must become.

An entrepreneur begins the process of defining success from the opposite direction, gravitating toward innovation, not emulation, as a way to achieve institutional excellence and sustainable competitive advantage. The entrepreneur defines success before attempting to measure it. After developing and articulating clear goals, an entrepreneur constructs a set of metrics that address the question, "How are we doing?"; the process begins by developing a strategy and a plan for implementing it. Most research universities have an overarching and compelling mission, often drafted decades or even centuries ago, that can easily be adapted to current realities. Similarly, many universities have identified a set of core values that shape their cultures (and, if not, that should be done). However it is in the area of strategy that entrepreneurial thinking can have the greatest impact. First, strategy is a plan for innovation, for being different. Without a strategy, universities are doomed to march in lockstep with their peers, engaging in a continuous contest for endowment and grants that allow them to outperform the competition and move up in the ratings. Second, strategy involves a set of concrete activities that, ideally, link with one another. If these activities are all executed well, they become hard to copy, creating a difference that is sustainable over time and therefore an alternative to simply running faster or longer than last year or working harder than the competition. Third, strategic activities can be rationalized throughout the university without imposing a one-size-fits-all approach. The strategic plans for the Law School, the College of Arts and Sciences, and the Journalism School can be very different, but they can all contribute to the successful execution of a university-wide strategy. Fourth, a good strategy is easily articulated so that buy-in can be obtained from the various constituencies that must support it if success is to be achieved. Typically it involves no more than four or at most five major initiatives, and with hard work each initiative can be reduced to no more than eight to ten words. Fifth, the results of a strategic plan lend themselves to simple metrics. A strategy can ultimately be translated to a dashboard that answers the question, "How are we doing?" The last reason to adopt a strategy is that it will favorably impact the external measures and rankings if it is the right one. Real institutional improvement is typically reflected in at least some of the popular measures of university success, and articulating a clear and convincing strategy can actually influence some of the metrics used by external sources in measuring the success of the university.

Great idea, but can you ever do it at a university? The autonomy granted to schools, departments, and even professors precludes a uniform approach to anything. Embedded in this concern is the suspicion among some that strategy is really just another word for imposing a kind of commercial discipline on the academic enterprise, placing economic concerns ahead of academic aspirations and changing for the worse the essential nature of the academy.

In fact, strategy is nothing more than a set of activities that interrelate with one another but when executed well can transform an institution. There is nothing uniform about the activities undertaken by each university unit and by each member of that unit in furtherance of an overall strategy. They don't have to be imposed from above but can be developed from the bottom up, as we will describe later in this chapter. Although not uniform, the activities should interrelate because they are guided by overall institutional goals and a strategic plan for achieving them. The broad strategic initiatives that make up the university-wide plan must be formulated through community-wide dialogue that reflects the values, strengths, and weaknesses of the institution. They can also be broad enough to leave latitude for creativity and diversity in the activities of academic units of all sizes.

What values are reflected in the overall institutional strategy unit is up to those involved in the process. Creating a strategy is simply a method for successfully implementing a set of values in an effective and sustainable way. For a research university, the most radical activity of all is to actually formulate an institutional strategy. The dialogue such a process fosters and the questions it raises will have a far-reaching and, we predict, positive impact.

We willingly acknowledge that a university community is a difficult place to develop and implement a strategic plan. The concerns likely to arise will be different at every institution, and many will be ones we haven't thought of; but we suspect a few themes will be virtually universal. There is a resistance to any approach that is not developed by consensus, a tall order at an institution as large and complex as a research university. This problem is compounded if the ultimate result is a set of bold strategic activities—not something that is ever arrived at by super-majority vote. A related issue is the problem of dual allegiances. The careers of typical faculty members are influenced as much by their standing among peers in their discipline as by their activity within the university. This often leads to departments and schools operating as independent fiefdoms that view campus-wide administration as an annoyance that has to be placated.

Developing a strategic planning process that is inclusive and transparent is critical to any hope that whatever is decided upon will gain broad acceptance. A stipulation at the outset that the final result will not be arrived at by majority vote but that all points of view will be considered should also help. In fact, encouragement of a wide range of ideas and points of view is critical to making the process work; this is a place where task forces and committees are of great value. Not only does such a stance increase the likelihood of community acceptance, but it also makes for a better result. Remember, strategy is about being different, and it is unlikely that bold, high-impact initiatives will emerge if unconventional thinking is not welcomed and embraced. No matter what approach is adopted, it will not be without its critics, but an inclusive process will minimize the criticism.

The most difficult hurdle involved in developing a strategy is not endemic to the university. It involves the concept of trade-off, or, said another way, deciding what not to do. In discussing strategy with successful leaders they uniformly stress the importance of focusing on a limited number of objectives, no matter how large and complex the enterprise. Recently, the president of one of the largest private foundations in the world told us his organization had three objectives and then explained he spent the preponderance of his time articulating them and maintaining internal focus. In any organization it is easier to try to do everything, and this is especially true in a university with an ethic built on consensus; but there is no hope for a successful strategy without trade-offs and making the choices that a strategic plan requires.

With a clear understanding that it won't be easy, we have some suggestions for developing a strategy and a plan for implementing it. The end result is clearly articulated, measurable university-wide goals together with measurable strategic initiatives that support the goals, a timeline, and, of course, a university-wide dashboard to answer the question, "How are we doing?" Similar goals and initiatives can be developed by the various components of the community, each with their own dashboard. Over time all members of the community would be part of a plan they could impact. With dashboards widely dispersed within schools, departments, and other initiatives, progress toward shared goals becomes transparent and all of the metrics roll up to the university-wide dashboard, which can also be widely disseminated as a regular report card. Admittedly, this vision is much too neat for a nonhierarchical community of highly educated individuals who chose academia, in part, so that others wouldn't tell them what to do. It does, however, have the advantage of being relatively clear and simple. The goals and aspirations of research universities are undoubtedly difficult to quantify, but we believe it is better for academics to develop reliable metrics than to have them imposed from the outside.

Using a university-wide dashboard as an end product, we want to walk through a hypothetical process we believe could achieve much of what we suggest.

The process begins with the appointment by the president of a relatively small planning body that reflects the seriousness of the undertaking and also the diverse groups that make up the university community. This group can have available to it the various studies, task force reports, and external reviews that are common in all research universities. The group then settles on a small number of university-wide goals and a limited number of strategic initiatives in support of each goal. The goals might address areas such as enrollment, teaching, institutional support, and research impact. The strategic initiatives would be activities that are institutionally specific and built upon unique university-wide strengths. Examples might include focused, merit-based recruitment programs or the encouragement of multidisciplinary teams that translate the most promising scientific research into sustainable solutions to problems of worldwide importance. The planning group would also develop a university-wide dashboard with measures for each goal such as the number of undergraduate applications for admission or the amount of total outside support, including sponsored research, private contributions, and other external contributions.

The next step is for the president to begin articulating the mission, values, and strategy of the university and asking other units in the university to develop plans to help achieve them. In response, each college and school undertakes a similar exercise. With a university-wide strategy as a guide, including clearly articulated and measurable goals, the process would result in a set of initiatives and activities that interlock both within each school and among them, and the metrics arrived upon would all roll up to the university-wide dashboard.

The university-wide enrollment goal illustrates how the process might work. The enrollment goal would be expressed in broad terms: "To attract a diverse group of world-class students to every educational unit of the university." The metric might be the number of targeted students actually enrolled, with special weighting going to graduate students, merit finalists, and other categories that have impact on the community beyond their absolute numbers. Every unit within the university would then have the opportunity to develop its own strategy for achieving this goal. For undergraduate admissions, it could be to target outstanding math and science students nationwide and enlist outstanding faculty as recruiters and mentors for these students. For the graduate school it could be a special fellowship aimed at students who have applied to departments or schools where their presence would have a high impact. The medical school could build on its preeminence in cancer research to attract graduate students and postdoctoral candidates with special promise in this area; and public health might take a similar tack in building on its worldwide reputation in the study of childhood obesity.

Some of these initiatives will work and others will have to be revised or abandoned. All can be measured and all can roll up to the university-wide goal. These activities relate to one another and if executed well will result in a focused, measurable, university-wide approach to improving the quality of the student body. In some cases the process might go even deeper, with departments such as economics, history, or applied science developing their own plans through the same process. Such departmental plans can serve as the basis for school-wide discussions on strategic alignment and will facilitate conversations on outputs and results because each plan will, by definition, include a dashboard.

Our hypothetical process takes at least two academic years: the first to develop and articulate a university strategy, and the second to develop the supporting strategic plans. Each plan should be dynamic and supported by an annual operating plan created as part of the budget process. Metrics are always a work in progress with new and more sophisticated measures growing out of the process. What doesn't change is the concept that every important enterprise in the community has a dashboard, and all of those doing the driving can answer the question, "How are we doing?"

11

The New Donors and University Development

A new breed of donors, both large and small, and the philanthropic institutions they have created and influence are exactly the constituency that is most attracted to our vision of the university as an engine of innovation, attacking the world's biggest problems with an entrepreneurial mindset. To the extent universities choose to move toward this vision these "new donors" should be willing supporters. It is unlikely, however, that universities can count on them to endow the status quo. It is with a sense of urgency that the new donors seek novel, valuable, high-impact solutions.

So who are the new donors and what do they choose to support? Ironically, they comprise both the most and least affluent segments of the university's donor pool, but both segments are worthy of attention. At the top they have been called "philanthro-capitalists." They are recently minted multimillionaires and billionaires represented by the likes of Bill Gates and Richard Branson. At the bottom are millions of individuals linked together in increasingly complex social networks who want to make a difference in the world by making small contributions on a regular basis using PayPal or their credit or debit cards. Together these two groups constitute a multibillion dollar constituency that universities must understand and be prepared to address. At the most basic level, the new donors are the customer of the future, and universities must have a product to sell them.

We will start with Bill Gates—just as most of us do every morning when we turn on our computers. It is increasingly apparent, however, that Microsoft is not the end of the story. In fact, Gates is destined to have a far bigger impact on the world as head of the Bill and Melinda Gates Foundation, the world's largest private foundation, than as the founder of the world's largest computer software company. Gates's ultimate impact will not come because of the vast resources at his disposal but from his revolutionary approach to giving. His philosophy has been evolving over at least a decade, but it crystallized in his first Annual Letter, written at the suggestion of his co-investor, Warren Buffett. It is a revealing and influential document about the new breed of philanthropists. Anyone aspiring to attack the world's biggest problems, whether they lead a country, a foundation, a university, a corporation, or a government agency can benefit from reading the Gates letter. That is exactly what we have done, not so much to unearth the workings and priorities of the Gates Foundation but to understand better the Gates approach and the mind of the new donor.

First, we sought to understand Gates's underlying motivations. What caused him to leave Microsoft and devote his full time to his foundation? He answers the question at the beginning of the letter. What excites him are: 1) opportunities for big breakthroughs; 2) building teams "with maniacal focus" that address tough problems; and 3) working with highly intelligent and dedicated people such as university scientists who have "critical knowledge and want to help make the breakthroughs."[1] The remainder of the letter illustrates his commitment to innovation, focus, leverage, and timely, measurable results. It also illustrates a willingness to admit mistakes, learn from them, and make midcourse corrections. Gates talks about the concept of leverage by linking the four main interests of the foundation: global health, global development, education in the United States, and basic research. He explains how these interests are interrelated; making progress in one area benefits the work taking place in the others. Gates also stresses the importance of strategy and a measurable action plan for implementation. In global health he articulates a clear direction: "Nothing on the planet saves children's lives more effectively and inexpensively than vaccines," and follows up with a plan that has measurable milestones to facilitate the development and distribution of vaccines that can cut childhood deaths from 10 million to 5 million in six years, adding a year to average life expectancy for well under one hundred dollars per person.[2] Returning to the concept of leverage, he suggests that progress on health issues can further the foundation's economic development goals because health and economic progress are interrelated. Gates understands that "when health improves . . . a virtuous cycle begins that takes a country out of poverty."[3] He highlights his interest in innovation when talking of agriculture and breakthroughs in the form of new seeds and fertilizer, but he immediately introduces a core belief that "technology is only useful if it helps people improve their lives, not as an end in itself." When it seeks to affect the course of basic scientific research—on which $90 billion of public and private funds is spent each year—the foundation endeavors to "make sure the new science is applied to the needs of the poor because the marketplace does not respond when the buyers have almost no money."[4] Gates prefers clear goals to platitudes. The foundation has set a rigorous four-to-six-year schedule to develop a pill or microbicide that will temporarily protect against HIV infection. But perhaps most extraordinary is Gates's discussion of failure. The $2 billion the foundation invested in American high schools over nine years fell short, in Gates's view, of its goal to increase numbers of college-ready graduates. Based on the data, he states that future efforts will focus on teacher effectiveness, the one variable that does seem to make a difference in educational outcomes.

The themes expressed in Gates's letter typify the attitudes of new donors and are further explained in two important books. In *Philanthro-Capitalism*, Matthew Bishop and Michael Green describe the growth of the newly affluent as well as their attitudes toward giving. Despite the recent economic downturn, data suggest that universities will continue to count new donors as an important part of their donor base. In *The Foundation: A Great American Secret*, Joel Fleishman explains how newly affluent individuals not only are establishing huge private foundations of their own to distribute their wealth but are also influencing the actions of older, more established foundations in directions consistent with the Gates letter.

Before the 1980s, new fortunes were relatively rare, but since then thousands of people have built assets of $100 million or more, and most made their money by starting their own companies and selling them. The philanthropy of these individuals, according to Bishop and Green, like that of Gates, is "market conscious," "impact oriented," often "high engagement," and always driven by the goal of maximizing the leverage of the donor's money.[5] Although there is only one Bill Gates, it is likely that virtually every research university will have a number of these new donors in their donor pool — self-made multimillionaires with a sense of urgency and a focused, hands-on approach to high-impact giving.

Private foundations have begun to take on the characteristics of new donors in part because many of them, like the Gates Foundation, were formed by wealthy young entrepreneurs and because the principles the new donors espouse are fast becoming best practices in the philanthropic world. In 2005, about 68,000 private foundations existed in the United States; their assets were estimated at half a trillion dollars and their annual grant making totaled $33.6 billion. Donor-directed community foundations control another $39 billion. After government, donor-directed vehicles will be the largest source of funds for research universities for the foreseeable future. Professor Fleishman's exhaustive study of the behavior of private foundations describes a "widespread emergence of a powerful new social conscience among many of the (newly) rich" who "are determined to make a difference." This movement toward what Fleishman calls "venture philanthropy" is also characterized by a hands-on grant-making style and a powerful focus on measurable results. Most important, Fleishman concludes that long-established foundations will evolve toward venture philanthropy because, in his words, "it is steadily becoming obvious that charitable dollars disbursed [in this way] . . . significantly overachieve in impact the dollars spent the old-fashioned way."[6]

The rise of philanthro-capitalism and venture philanthropy will impact the fundraising environment in which research universities operate in a number of ways. Gifts will be strongly shaped by a strategy and a point of view. The Gates letter is a great example. Any institution hoping for support from the Gates Foundation must understand the mind of Bill Gates and propose initiatives that not only meet program guidelines but are consistent with the philosophical approach Gates outlines. For most of the new donors, there will be no annual letter, but there will be a Gatesian point of view. Connecting with them will require more than tailoring existing activities to a particular template. More fundamental steps will be required. New donors want to invest, not just give, and they want to invest in solutions to big problems. They want their investments to leverage other resources so that impact can be increased. They want relentless focus and measurable results. All indicators point to the fact that these demands will come not only from new donors but, increasingly, from traditional foundations and even governments. Universities have all of the pieces needed to satisfy the demands of the new donors, but, as we have emphasized throughout this book, it takes a commitment to innovation, an entre-preneurial mindset, and an unquenchable desire to execute.

New donors also have short time horizons. They are impatient—a trait that has often rewarded them handsomely in the private sector. These personality characteristics have significant implications for the initiatives they undertake. Almost all of the new foundations created in the last fifteen years are sunset foundations designed to spend themselves out of existence within a fixed period of time. This is a dramatic change from the old foundation model. In the entire twentieth century, less than fifty American foundations actually spent themselves out of existence. This new model means institutions are going to be on a short leash and donors are going to be very engaged as they seek to achieve specific goals within a definite time frame.

In his letter, Gates wonders if the devotion of more resources will lead to faster results; this question is typical of new donors, who are focused more on solving a problem and less on establishing in-perpetuity foundations. Related to this impulse toward impact and results is the desire to scale encouraging projects and initiatives to grow beyond their original vision. The first question a new donor is likely to ask after a project has achieved initial success is if it can be grown so that it has a greater impact nationally or even internationally. If the model is correct, the answer will be, "Yes, if we have enough money." It often takes many years before that answer is truly accurate. Without question, there is a downside to the impatience of the new donors. The kind of basic research or scholarship that often forms the basis for innovation will not typically be funded by results-oriented entrepreneurs, at least not without a major educational effort on the part of university leaders. That kind of research will most likely be funded by more patient government money with the expectation that breakthroughs in basic science and traditional scholarship will result in greater investment by donors with a shorter time horizon.

Because the new donors are less concerned about creating in-perpetuity funds than solving a large, intractable problem, they often look askance at providing funds for endowment. They think of endowment funds as "lazy money" because typically only 5 percent of the total gift can be employed in any one year. If you want to end world poverty or cure cancer in your own lifetime, the endowment model simply does not work. We are not convinced impatience is all bad. There will always be a pool of legacy donors who want to give back to an institution they love, and endowed professorships, buildings, or programs are the vehicle of choice; U.S. higher education would not be where it is without these vehicles. But new departments and permanent centers are not always the best way to attack tough problems. High-impact, innovative, and entrepreneurial research and scholarship are, by definition, constantly evolving. The leaders behind such research are also likely to tolerate higher degrees of risk. Evolving configurations with sunset provisions are often a better approach for this kind of work, and these forms are precisely tailored to the expendable gifts that appeal to new donors.

A variety of institutional initiatives can be supported by expendable funds and still have substantial institutional impact. Merit-based scholarships are an example. At our own institution, an innovative approach to attracting great students to UNC and Duke and providing them with the best that both communities have to offer is supported with expendable funds. Lastly, we see a hybrid model developing where problem-based short-term programs evolve over time (usually ten years or more) into organizational forms that are appropriate for perpetual endowment; and the original donor is often so involved and committed to the idea that she provides the gift for endowment. The hybrid might also involve a mix of endowment and expendable funds in an effort to attract support from both affluent givers and the large number of small givers we discuss later in this chapter.

You cannot talk to one of the new donors for long without discussing metrics. In the Gates letter, metrics emerge on the third page with the comment, "I hope you didn't think you were going to get through this letter without some figures being thrown at you," and that comment is followed with two graphs. Initiatives that appeal to philanthrocapitalists have precise, measurable goals, and their leaders can provide clear answers when asked, "How are we doing?" The dashboard is a useful starting point in responding to the need for metrics, which can't be developed without a clear set of goals and a strategy. Once goals and strategy are in place, three to five indices of success can be developed, tracked, and modified as necessary. The answer, "We can't measure success, but we will know when we get there," is unacceptable. The entrepreneurs who are typically new donors have heard that answer all too often during their careers and accepting it inevitably resulted in disaster. These metrics do not have to be perfect, and they can be modified over time. They do have to be in place at the outset, and there must be buy-in as to their value if the new donor is to invest capital and time in university-based projects and enterprises.

Historically, small donors have been important to university development, but it is not clear how to engage them fully. Annual fund drives directed by junior development officers, including class gifts or "friends" campaigns for the library or minor sports programs are often the only efforts aimed at the bottom of the potential donor pool. This is the case for three reasons. First, the process of reaching these donors is time consuming and expensive, and the dollars collected, though immediately expendable, are relatively small. Second, there is a general bias against small, expendable contributions in university development offices that have huge campaign goals that are typically met by large, one-time gifts. Third, the stories universities have to tell have rarely been communicated in a way that competes with more immediate and perhaps more compelling opportunities. An article in the *New York Times* questioning the wisdom of a class reunion gift to Harvard's general endowment at a time when eliminating extreme poverty seemed more urgent demonstrates the conflict many donors feel between university and charitable giving.[7] Harvard's reluctance to redirect the class gift to other causes ultimately became a public relations nightmare.

As universities focus more on problem-based, high-impact research designed to address big problems, they address the concerns of the large new donors. Such research also appeals to donors making smaller contributions who are concerned about making a difference in the world. Any doubt about the importance of this group and the huge opportunity they afford should have been answered during the course of the political campaign of 2008. Astonishing results can be achieved when a message that appeals to these donors is coupled with evolving trends in social networking and always-on telecommunications tools. Though figures differ, it is clear that the Obama campaign raised close to $115 million from donors giving less than $200.[8] The astounding sums raised from small donors in the election focused attention on a phenomenon that has been emerging for some time and can best be characterized as online philanthropy. Using websites such as Kickstarter and GlobalGiving, activists in their twenties and thirties have been raising funds for their favorite causes for several years now. Sites such as Donors Choose and Kiva not only promote attractive causes but also allow contributors to connect directly to recipients. Kiva, a microlending site, has, as of September 2009, attracted nearly half a million lenders who together have contributed more than $62 million.[9] Online giving is nothing new to universities. We couldn't find an American research university that didn't have a website encouraging online contributions. But giving to the library or the field hockey team—or even the English Department—seems passive and remote when compared to providing mosquito nets for children in Somalia or making loans to women in Bangladesh. The university as an engine of innovation will appeal to new donors by focusing on problems, solutions, impact, and urgency.

Our experience with one large donor and some nascent thoughts about reaching donors making smaller contributions suggests an approach to the new giving paradigm. Gary Parr is a graduate of the University of North Carolina from the small town of Burlington, North Carolina. His grandfather, Lawrence "Lefty" Wilson, pitched for the UNC baseball team from 1918 to 1922. After graduating from UNC in 1979 and immediately obtaining an MBA, Gary went to work in finance, soon becoming an expert in structuring financial institutions of all kinds. Currently the vice chair of Lazard, the New York investment banking firm, he has been deeply involved in the restructuring of the world's financial institutions over the last several years. Typical of the new donors, Parr had something he wanted to accomplish at UNC. After several long conversations with Professor Ruel Tyson, the religion professor and founder of the Institute for the Arts and Humanities whom we introduced in Chapter 5, Parr became committed to establishing ethics as an important component of the undergraduate experience. Initially, he worked with the Business School to establish an ethics course for undergraduates with the thought the course might evolve into a more elaborate curriculum and eventually spread to the campus as a whole. For a variety of reasons, this first attempt didn't meet Parr's expectations, and he decided to try a different approach. After multiyear discussions with Professor Tyson, Parr met Geoffrey Sayre-McCord, the chair of the Philosophy Department, and one of those magical partnerships between an academic and an entrepreneur was born. In Parr's view, the Philosophy Department was not perceived as a threat or a competitor by any other department or school, and therefore it could serve as a facilitator, bringing together interdepartmental resources to focus upon ethical questions in the arts, sciences, and professions. In 2004, after ten years of experimentation, he established the Parr Center for Ethics with both endowment and expendable funds. But that was only the beginning. Parr has stayed deeply involved in the center and has constantly pushed for it to scale its efforts and increase its impact inside the university and within the state. Unwilling to limit its activities solely to teaching, the center is now focusing on the ethical issues raised by biotechnology and other advances in medicine, collaborating with traditional scientists, doctors, and the School of Public Health. Justifiably proud of the

Parr Center's achievements to date, Parr wants more definitive plans for growth and has assembled an impressive advisory board to suggest future directions. As those directions evolve, there is reason to be optimistic about Parr's continuing involvement and support.

We take away four important lessons from the university's experience with Gary Parr. First, it is necessary to understand the goals and motivations of the donor from the beginning and stay engaged as they change over time. Large donors like Parr will likely be focused on a problem, and the more measurable progress that can be achieved the more involved and committed the donor. Second, start small and take some risks with expendable funds and maximum donor involvement until a sustainable model emerges. Third, match the donor with an entrepreneurially oriented academic who can meet the donor halfway and form a partnership that provides both academic credibility and a sense of urgency and purpose consistent with the donor's mindset. Fourth, understand that the process will probably take ten years and there will be some failures along the way. If everyone involved understands these lessons from the outset and embraces and even celebrates the ups and the downs of the endeavor, it has a higher likelihood of success.

With respect to attracting smaller new donors our thinking is less evolved because we, like most in our position, are new to this area. At this point, the best we can do is to explain how we think about the opportunity. When we log on to a typical university online giving site, we are offered the opportunity to support one of the following: colleges or schools within the university; an initiative such as the University Fund, Class Gift, or Women and Philanthropy; or a special area such as the library or the alumni association. Compare that with the Internet site created by Change.org, an organization aimed expressly at small donors. Here the person chooses between encouraging social entrepreneurship by providing a ten dollar laptop in India, encouraging fair trade by supporting coffee cooperatives in Ethiopia, and addressing homelessness in the United States by helping homeless veterans. Obviously, the traditional university offerings do not compete. The passion and enthusiasm that jumps off the page at Change.org, Kiva, or Donors Choose is uniformly missing from university online giving. The social networking that has proven so effective in encouraging online giving is missing as well. Again, the projects, initiatives, and ways of thinking that correspond to the aspirations and mindsets of the large new donors will help address the issues we raise here. Problem-based, high-impact research can be translated into opportunities that attract small donors. Creating the right projects with compelling descriptions will probably require a different point of view from the one that currently pervades the leadership of a typical development office; younger staff members clearly understand the opportunity. This isn't about serving the highly affluent. It is about changing the world and enlisting our recent graduates to help us.

We have undertaken a few small steps in that direction. Our entrepreneurship minor is developing a website in cooperation with one of the students who recently graduated from the program and formed a website development company. He believes he can translate the lessons he learned in the private sector to a site that can keep recent graduates of the program connected and committed. The goal is obtaining support for a portion of the program's yearly operating budget from graduates. If this effort achieves some success, we will seek to build on it with a decentralized, under-the-radar, bottom-up approach, which is how such efforts typically begin. Once we figure it out, perhaps there will be an opportunity to scale the project to include more programs and initiatives. In the interim, we encourage our peers to experiment in this area as well. Those universities that actually become engines of innovation and routinely impact the world's biggest problems will also be able to generate an increasing portion of their total expendable contributions online.

The philosopher Alfred North Whitehead said, "Universities create the future"; and Drew Gilpin Faust, president of Harvard, explained that they do so "in two fundamental ways: by educating those to whom the future belongs, and by generating the ideas and discoveries that can transform the present and build a better world."[1] Despite unprecedented challenges we remain enthusiastic about the role of research universities at this moment in history—perhaps because as entrepreneurs we habitually see opportunity when confronted with adversity.

The challenges are real, and daunting. On average, university endowments are 30 percent smaller than they were at the beginning of the financial crisis, and the situation is much worse for many of the institutions whose budgets depend on state funds. Whether voluntarily or involuntarily, universities must reinvent themselves and at the same time respond to the most serious problems of our day. Universities are being asked to do more precisely at a time when their resources are dramatically constricting. In such an environment, it is not possible simply to throw money at emerging problems. Rather, students and faculty must discard traditional notions of academic compartmentalization and resource availability and view themselves as members of teams capable of mobilizing on their own initiative and prepared to leverage resources beyond the walls of their own institutions.

This requirement that research universities do more with less convinces us that an entrepreneurial mindset is required for these great institutions to have the impact we know they can. An environment of rapid change, like the one we confront today, demands innovation, and entrepreneurial thinking increases the impact of innovative ideas. As research universities take on society's biggest challenges, it is imperative that we expand the conversation beyond the walls of academia and make entrepreneurs and entrepreneurial thinking part of the dialogue.

Achieving these goals will require a different process on every campus. One size will not fit all. We have provided some examples of effective programs and ways of working, but we don't have a prescription for success. We believe the real challenge is to create a campus culture that is respectful of the university and its traditional strengths while embracing ways of thinking that are not always found in an academic environment. Ultimately, we hope we have provided not a detailed map but a compass to hold us to our fundamental values while pointing us toward high-impact teaching and research.

As we have said, innovation is central to the road ahead for research universities, and entrepreneurial thinking increases the likelihood that such innovation will be successful. But we also recognize that injecting an entrepreneurial point of view into an academic environment is easier said than done. The initial challenge is to chart a course that embraces the ideals of a research university while still being anchored in the practical world of step-by-step execution. Most universities have mission statements that point to a noble purpose, but an inspiring mission without an actionable and measurable plan will achieve little. Striking a balance between rhetoric and action often requires a unique point of view and a set of life experiences that traditional academics might characterize as "different." However, combining execution with innovation is exactly what we have advocated throughout this work. Entrepreneurial thinking is often the missing ingredient that, when added to the ideas and discoveries generated by the academy, translates grand visions into reality.

An equally important challenge pits those who believe that the purpose of a great university is the pursuit of knowledge for its own sake against those who believe that only research that can be applied to real-world problems is worthy of support. This debate has gone on since the founding of the University of Padua in 1222 and continues unabated to this day. An entrepreneurial approach suggests a "third way" between engagement and disengagement. Entrepreneurs begin with a problem to be solved or a customer to be satisfied and then, without regard to preexisting constraints, seek to marshal the resources required to achieve the goal. As we discussed earlier, this marshaling and repurposing of resources can take the form of "creative destruction." In a university context, we would characterize it as selective destruction. Selective because the disciplines that form the heart of any academic institution must remain vital and strong if they are to provide the knowledge and talent required to attack the big problems that a great university is compelled by its mission to confront. At the same time, the silo mentality that inhibits interdisciplinary cooperation must give way.

As we have argued, interdisciplinary combinations of all kinds require well-trained recruits and talented leaders. It is up to the core disciplines to provide the talent as well as to engage in the basic research and unfettered academic activity that support problem-based initiatives. At the same time, it should be clear that attacking large problems requires multidisciplinary collaborations small and large, ranging from ad hoc task forces to recombined departments. An entrepreneurial approach favors combinations that focus directly on the problems they seek to solve, combinations that can be easily realigned. This is where the notion of an entrepreneurial culture becomes important. To entrepreneurs, neither lifetime employment nor perpetual institutions are a high priority, and closing or mothballing disappointing initiatives is not only acceptable but, at times, worth celebrating. When entrepreneurial thinking becomes part of the culture of a great university, problem solving can comfortably take place beside more traditional forms of inquiry. All kinds of problem-based combinations can complement the traditional disciplinary structures. And when the university is not the best agent for adding impact to innovation in a particular case, the right partner or external agent to carry out the idea can be quickly identified.

Finally, to make innovation and entrepreneurship part of the fabric of research universities, there must be room for entrepreneurs inside the institution. In some cases this means the inclusion of individuals who have led or been involved with entrepreneurial projects or initiatives. In other instances, it involves embracing a mindset that regards change as an opportunity to undertake difficult challenges without all of the required resources in hand. University trustees should be open to choosing entrepreneurs or entrepreneurial thinkers for leadership positions, and entrepreneurs should be recruited as both full-time and adjunct faculty members. There is also a great opportunity to teach faculty the specific skills and the mentality required to approach problems as opportunities and turn ideas into reality. We are not suggesting that all faculty or even all university leaders should be entrepreneurs. Rather, we are suggesting that entrepreneurs be sprinkled in the mix, ideally throughout the university community. When this happens, not only does the work of the university have more impact, but the culture of the university begins to change.

As is the case in most of the world's important institutions in these challenging times, the lifting will only get heavier for us and our colleagues throughout higher education. Expectations are high and resources are constrained. Though the task is daunting, we have confidence in the ability and the commitment of our colleagues and our students. We are also more convinced than ever that the road ahead for universities demands an entrepreneurial spirit and the involvement of entrepreneurs, who are optimists at heart, who think big thoughts, and who are not afraid to fail because they have failed before and lived to tell the tale.

The dialogue surrounding *Engines of Innovation* began in Chapel Hill with a daylong, campus-wide symposium in October of 2010, attended by roughly 100 faculty members from throughout our university. The discussion continued in a variety of academic and nonacademic settings and in large groups and small, as well as in the local and national media. From CNBC to a panel at the German Embassy in Washington, D.C., and at universities and colleges large and small, we had the chance to learn more about the ideas we suggest in *Engines* from a remarkable group of colleagues and friends. We've also had the chance to implement many of the ideas we discuss based upon an Innovation Roadmap developed by a group of UNC faculty, alumni, and students (http://innovate.unc.edu/site/wp-content/uploads/2012/10/Innovate_at_Carolina_Roadmap.pdf). The rapid change in the landscape of higher education over the last three years could justify an entirely new volume, but, as we said in our preface, the basic principles we discuss in *Engines* are still valid, at least from our point of view, and so this chapter should be seen as an update. In it we want to discuss the four themes we think are most important as we assess the current environment.

There Is Opportunity at the Intersection of the Liberal Arts and Technology

The idea from the book that has generated the most interest is the concept of broadening the notion of academic entrepreneurship to include fields outside of science and engineering. The iconic image of Steve Jobs standing under two intersecting street signs, one reading "technology" and the other "liberal arts," helped us understand that much of what we wrote in *Engines* about breaking down academic silos centers upon a profound relationship between technology and the arts and sciences. The relationship between technology and both physical and social science is self-evident. Virtually all serious scientific undertakings we know about have a significant information technology component, and with the advent of what has become known as "big data," this trend has become even more pronounced. The relationship between the liberal arts and technology is more subtle, but we believe it's equally important. To begin with, our great universities are the only institutions in our society where world-class technologists work in direct proximity with world-class humanists. We have learned that when they get together fascinating things can happen. The campus-wide symposium to discuss *Engines* was led by the chair of the History Department, and in one panel he asserted that if entrepreneurs were destined to confront failure, they should study history, because history "is the department of failure." At the same time, the entirely new field of the digital humanities has emerged, with new academic journals and serious research tools popping up monthly. Our own UNC colleague Bobby Allen recently received a significant grant from the Andrew W. Mellon Foundation to create a digital humanities lab that helps scholars turn huge amounts of historical data into patterns that explain economic and social change within discrete geographic communities. This digital trend has also found its way into even more esoteric fields such as literary criticism.[1]

To explore the relationship between the arts and technology even further we decided to teach a survey course in the fall of 2012, open to all students, called "Introduction to Entrepreneurship" (Econ 125) and anchor it at the intersection of the liberal arts and technology. The inspiration for the course grew out of a conversation with a first-year student from China who said, "Before I connect the dots I need to collect the dots." Our task was first to determine the dots that needed to be collected and second to clearly relate the dots to the subject of entrepreneurship. We designed a broad survey course that included history, where the focus was dramatic and devastating failure; philosophy, where the subject was the moral risk associated with entrepreneurship; and economics, where the focus was on the role of entrepreneurship as the research and development function for an entire economy. We also included some of the basic skills any entrepreneur needs to know about, such as accounting, marketing, design, and strategy. Different forms of entrepreneurship—social, commercial, artistic, scientific, and academic—were also discussed.

Each class began with an important piece of music and an explanation of why it was important. We involved numerous guest lecturers, including Michael Porter, Wendy Kopp, Steve Case, Bob Langer, and Bob Gaudio (a songwriter and performer who is one of the original Four Seasons), as well as preeminent academics and entrepreneurs. The class began with 360 students and, after a difficult midterm exam, settled at about 320. It was held in a state-of-the-art classroom loaded with technology, enabling students to interact with the instructors and the lecturers from their laptops and phones and to answer quiz questions at the end of every class from their laptops or smartphones. Students also engaged in a class project, which resulted in roughly seventy different teams producing videos on the subject "What's the Big Idea?" Much to our surprise, the projects were well executed, and course evaluations rated the projects as the outstanding part of the class, notwithstanding the fact that little class time was devoted to them and they comprised only 10 percent of the final grade.

On the first day of class we announced that the 2012 version would be "Class 1.0" and next year's version would be better. On this point we are more convinced than ever. In post-semester evaluations 64 percent of the class said it had a major impact on decisions they will make about their life and 55 percent said the class would influence their future course of study. An articulate minority of students, however, concluded that the linkages between entrepreneurship, technology, and the liberal arts remained unclear and the experiential aspect of the class should be emphasized and better integrated into the class content. In short, we made a good start but have a long way to go.

Our first semester teaching a large introductory class on innovation and entrepreneurship has convinced us that there is huge opportunity at the intersection of the liberal arts and technology and that entrepreneurship connects the two subjects. Our experience supports one of the central themes of this book: entrepreneurship is not a discipline or a specific set of skills but a way of thinking—and entrepreneurial thinking can be taught. Most important, our experience with this large class reinforces our conviction that if students can learn to think like entrepreneurs, in the broadest sense, high-level innovation and execution will follow.

Online Education Will Dramatically Reshape the Classroom

The state of online education in early 2013 is reminiscent of the state of the Internet in 2000. There is a huge amount of excitement, a plethora of competing models, and an inordinate amount of hand-wringing about the impact these new models will have on existing educational institutions. We believe the strong naysayers and the true believers are both wrong: even the most skilled futurists could not predict all of the winners and losers from the early days of the Internet boom (or bubble, depending on your perspective) but, notwithstanding the hype, most of us underestimated the impact of the World Wide Web. We think the same applies to online education, and at the beginning of 2012, we began a process of understanding it better.

As with other important problems we have tackled, our default approach is to start with the customer, in this case our students. We decided the best way to learn about online education was to teach the large introductory course described above with a twist. We persuaded a colleague in the Department of Communications Studies to teach a seminar that studied and filmed our class. The seminar also surveyed all of the competing online course models, the best-of-breed individual classes, and the costs associated with producing a great online experience. The seminar participants also involved Google in the conversation in an effort to understand best practices and how to use cutting-edge technology to enhance the online experience.

By the end of the 2012 fall semester we had in hand the following: video covering twenty hours of course lectures and a short trailer for each lecture, a set of recommendations for the future of our course from the seminar, a comprehensive course survey completed by more than 300 students, the results of a small focus group that included students who were doing well and not so well in our survey course, and an invitation from the university to submit a proposal and budget to turn "Introduction to Entrepreneurship" into a MOOC (Massive Open Online Course).

While we haven't yet made a firm decision about the direction for our own course, we have reached some conclusions about our experience so far and the implications it has for teaching in the context of a research university. First, for classes like ours, where active participation is essential to learning (entrepreneurship is a contact sport), the actual and virtual classrooms are interconnected and can enhance one another. For example, the twenty hours of video lectures produced as supplemental material for a MOOC can also be content for our traditional class, allowing students to view lectures in advance. Technology enables the large classroom to become more interactive, with a lively dialogue between students, instructors, and outside speakers the standard mode of operation. Similarly, techniques developed to foster interactivity in the classroom can, we believe, be adapted to enhance the online experience, which is essential if the class being offered is not designed to teach simply hard skills but rather a way of thinking that must be practiced in order to be mastered.

Second, alternatives to traditional testing and certification must be developed, because a disproportionate amount of time and energy is currently being spent on this, at the expense of student learning. We think we stumbled onto one approach to this problem that has potential. As we have already discussed, the seventy student projects consisting of an online video on the subject "What's the Big Idea?" far exceeded our expectations and, for the most part, provided real insight into what the student team had learned in our class. The video itself might well be a better certificate than a heavily proctored multiple-choice test or even an essay. (Our multiple-choice tests received low marks from our students, who asked that the project comprise a much larger part of their final grade.) Replacing traditional testing with demonstrable evidence of proficiency could be a solution to the problems associated with evaluating student performance in MOOCs, and the lessons learned can be carried over to the more traditional classroom.

Third, the most promising framework for MOOCs and online education in general—the use of social media and other online tools to foster intimate interaction on a worldwide scale—is still unrealized. Literally hundreds or even thousands of class projects, online study groups, and other work groups can be facilitated using existing and emerging tools, and the diversity of the groups themselves is potentially unprecedented. The mechanics of such an endeavor are daunting, but the potential to build classes that routinely involve teams with members that span the globe engaged in conversations that would be impossible without emerging social media tools makes the hard work of implementation worth the effort. We suspect that the subject we have chosen to focus upon, innovation and entrepreneurship, is an ideal proving ground for testing our beliefs about the importance of online education, and we look forward to doing so.

Simplifying Licensing Policies Can Increase the Rate of Company Formation

University leaders are very familiar with complaints about how difficult it is for startup companies to license university technology. These complaints are often founded in reality—it does take a long time to get these deals done. Some of the reasons are the fault of the university: technology transfer officers want good terms for their employers, the deals often require the approval of officers with full calendars that are difficult to schedule, and the faculty member who is the founder of the company is a valued colleague who needs to be dealt with carefully. On the company side, it may be unclear precisely what the business model will be, which makes the value difficult to assess; financing may be uncertain, which raises questions about how patent costs and other up-front expenses will be covered; and the early management team may not have experience at negotiating complex licenses.

At UNC-Chapel Hill, we addressed this problem through the creation of standard license agreements for different sectors that represented reasonable estimates of where these negotiations would end. The resulting process, called the Carolina Express License, allows startup companies to execute a standard license quickly, often in days. Prior to the use of the Carolina Express License, these negotiations took months or even years. Twenty UNC startups have now been created using this process, which has dramatically accelerated company formation. The express license recognizes that most startups will not have significant capital upon formation, so the reimbursement of patent costs is delayed six months, and there are no up-front payments.

In addition to producing more companies, this approach generates much greater satisfaction among faculty members who are company founders. The negotiations that lead to company formation can be the source of bad feelings that linger for a long time. This streamlined approach shortens the negotiation process and reduces the likelihood of faculty dissatisfaction. The disadvantages of the express license are that the lack of up-front payments sometimes leads to less urgency for the company to raise money, which can delay the reimbursement of patent costs even further, and that the university loses the opportunity to press for a better deal when a particularly exciting venture that might already have funding comes along.

We believe the advantages of the standard license outweigh the disadvantages. Carnegie Mellon University reached a similar conclusion in developing its "Five Percent, Go in Peace" policy, which predates the Carolina Express License. Nevertheless, the critics of these policies, who believe the university leaves money on the table by not meticulously negotiating an optimum deal, have a point. The university has provided the faculty member with employment, with a lab to work in, with grants management support, with an educational platform to attract students and postdocs, and much more, and the university does deserve to be compensated for these things. But as a practical matter, the faculty member who wants his or her career enhanced and fulfilled by the experience of starting a company does not go through this calculus. Neither does the public that wants to see more tangible outcomes from university research. So, balancing all of these things, a standard license strategy is warranted. To our knowledge, no other university has adopted a similar strategy since Carolina adopted the express license.

Universities Must Prepare Students for Jobs That Don't Exist Yet

A prolonged recession resulting in unacceptable levels of unemployment among recent college graduates has given rise to legitimate concern about whether universities are adequately preparing students for a job upon graduation.[2] If the test is whether universities impart entry-level skills that are useful in a variety of jobs and professions, the answer depends on what major a student pursues. A degree in journalism or business may translate more easily into a job than a degree in history or English. However, we believe research universities play a unique role in preparing students for jobs that don't even exist yet, and that is a sustainable competitive advantage for higher education.

Guessing at the specific skills that will make a first-year student employable upon graduation is sheer folly in an environment where even venerable companies and institutions evolve so rapidly that in four years they are hardly recognizable. What is certain is that the flavor of this week—be it search engine optimization, crowdsourcing, or mobile applications—will be supplanted by something new, and incoming first-year students may know more than their professors about these latest developments. On the other hand, as we have suggested repeatedly in this book, universities are well suited to train students in particular disciplines, problem solving, and ways of thinking that will allow them to participate in the innovative and rapidly evolving economy that awaits them. An actual example proves our point. One student we know majored in sociology and wrote her senior paper on arranged marriage in India, based on extensive fieldwork on the subject. The specific skills she acquired through this endeavor prepared her for only one career, that of an academic sociologist. Upon graduation, however, she moved to New York to become a writer, paying the bills by working as a proofreader while taking courses at night on how to get published. Within a year she was hired as a blog editor for the Huffington Post (blogs didn't exist when she was a first-year student), a job that led to opportunities as both a writer and an editor. All of her jobs to date have been with online publications, and there is some chance she will never work for an enterprise that puts words on paper. This student's experience is replicated over and over, not only in newly founded enterprises and industries but in established ones as well. The specific skills that will be required four years hence for an entry-level job at General Motors or General Electric are also impossible to predict, and executives at companies such as these tell us they are looking for problem solvers who can communicate effectively, the kind of people universities are particularly well suited to produce.

Even if universities could predict the future, as institutions they are not particularly well suited to prepare students for their first jobs. For the most part, the entry-level skills university professors understand best are those associated with becoming a university professor. The skills that allow faculty to excel in creating new knowledge and solving large, complex problems do not easily translate into a first job, and to reinvent universities to become job-training institutions would negate much of what, we believe, makes them important and unique. It would destroy the philosophy that we feel has distinguished the United States from the rest of the world for all of its history: of the thirty-five U.S. presidents who went to college, only three were science majors. The liberal arts education has defined America, including its high-tech economy. Providing a liberal arts education in a research university, teeming with new ideas, innovations, and innovators, fuels the entrepreneurial spirit in our graduates at a time in our nation's history when just such an impulse is needed.

The risk of writing a chapter that assesses the current environment and focuses on important trends is that it is out of date the minute it is published. We suggest that the conversation should continue. Although our destination is uncertain, we can promise the process of getting there will be eventful and at times dramatic. We look forward to the road ahead.

NOTES

Introduction

1. Eric Schmidt, interview by Kai Ryssdal, *Marketplace*, American Public Media, July 7, 2009.
2. Michael Porter, "Why America Needs an Economic Strategy," *Business Week*, October 30, 2008.
3. Gerald F. Seib, "In Crisis, Opportunity for Obama," *Wall Street Journal*, November 21, 2008.
4. Porter, "Why America Needs an Economic Strategy."
5. Henry Rosovsky, "Two Thirds of the Best," in *The University: An Owner's Manual* (New York: Norton, 1990), 29–36.
6. Peter F. Drucker, *Innovation and Entrepreneurship: Practice and Principles* (New York: Harper Business, 1993), 23.
7. Frank H. T. Rhodes, *The Creation of the Future: The Role of the American University* (Ithaca, N.Y.: Cornell University Press, 2001), 5.
8. Drucker, *Innovation and Entrepreneurship*, 23.
9. Elizabeth D. Capaldi et al., "The Top American Research Universities, 2008 Annual Report," Center for Measuring University Performance, http://mup.asu.edu/research2008.pdf (accessed August 20, 2009).
10. Richard L. Florida, *The Rise of the Creative Class: And How It's Transforming Work, Leisure, Community and Everyday Life* (New York: Basic Books, 2002).
11. Ronald G. Ehrenberg, ed., *The American University: National Treasure or Endangered Species?* (Ithaca, N.Y.: Cornell University Press, 1997).
12. Our colleague Jonathan Cole has eloquently made this point throughout his monumental work, *The Great American University: Its Rise to Preeminence, Its Indispensable National Role, Why It Must Be Protected* (New York: PublicAffairs, 2009).
13. Drucker, *Innovation and Entrepreneurship*, 26.
14. Ibid., 33.

Chapter 1

1. "College and University Endowments Over $250 Million, 2008," *Chronicle of Higher Education*, August 24, 2009.
2. John Kao, *Innovation Nation: How America Is Losing Its Innovation Edge, Why It Matters, and What We Can Do to Get It Back* (New York: Free Press, 2007), 24.
3. Ibid., 25.
4. Morley Winograd and Michael D. Hais, *Millennial Makeover: MySpace,*

YouTube, and the Future of American Politics (New Brunswick, N.J.: Rutgers University Press, 2008), 142.

5. Kao, *Innovation Nation*, 159.

6. Ibid.

7. ActBlue, "About ActBlue," http://www.actblue.com/about (accessed August 20, 2009).

8. Katharine Q. Seelye and Leslie Wayne, "The Web Takes Ron Paul for a Ride," *New York Times*, November 11, 2007.

9. Jose Antonio Vargas, "Obama Raised Half a Billion Online," *Washington Post*, November 20, 2008.

10. Deloitte Consulting, "Who Are the Millennials?" http://www.deloitte .com/dtt/cda/doc/content/us_consulting_millennialfactsheet_080606 .pdf (accessed August 20, 2009); Winograd and Hais, *Millennial Makeover*, 67; ibid., 82; Deloitte Consulting, "Who Are the Millennials?"

11. Reynot Junco and Jeanna Mastrodicasa, *Connecting to the Net.Generation: What Higher Education Professionals Need to Know about Today's Students* (Washington, D.C.: National Association of Student Personnel Administrators, 2007).

12. Kao, *Innovation Nation*, 38–39.

13. Congressional Research Service, "Federal Research and Development Funding: FY 2007," Report for Congress, updated October 10, 2006, http:// www.fas.org/sgp/crs/misc/RL33345.pdf (accessed August 20, 2009).

14. Marisa Lopez-Rivera, "Update on Billion-Dollar Campaigns at 33 Institutions," *Chronicle of Higher Education*, August 6, 2009.

15. Kao, *Innovation Nation*, 133.

Chapter 2

1. Ronda Britt, "Universities Report Continued Decline in Real Federal S&E R&D Funding in FY 2007," National Science Foundation website, http:// www.nsf.gov/statistics/infbrief/nsf08320/ (accessed August 20, 2009).

2. "The Gates Challenge for Global Health," *Seattle Times*, May 19, 2005.

3. Stuart Pfeifer and Tom Petruno, "Support Keeps Growing for a Milken Pardon," AllBusiness.com, February 8, 2009, http://www.allbusiness .com/government/government-bodies-offices/12032830-1.html (accessed April 5, 2010); "America's Most Generous Donors," *The Chronicle of Philanthropy*, http://philanthropy.com/stats/donors/detail.php?ID_Gift=1975 (accessed August 20, 2009).

4. H. Kent Bowen, Alex Kazaks, Ayr Muir-Harmony, and Bryce LaPierre, "The Langer Lab: Commercializing Science," *Harvard Business Publishing Brief Cases*, March 2, 2005, 10; ibid., 11; ibid., 13.

5. Langer Lab website, "Home" and "Research," http://web.mit.edu/langerlab/ index.html (accessed August 20, 2009).

6. Bowen, Kazaks, Muir-Harmony, and LaPierre, "The Langer Lab," 5.

7. Ibid., 17

8. Joseph DeSimone (Chancellor's Eminent Professor of Chemistry, University of North Carolina at Chapel Hill; William R. Kenan Jr. Distinguished Professor of Chemical Engineering, North Carolina State University; principal investigator, DeSimone Research Group), in discussion with Goldstein, September 8, 2008.

9. Ibid.

10. Andlinger Center for Energy and the Environment website, "Gift of $100 million to transform energy and environment research at Princeton," July 1, 2008, http://www.princeton.edu/acee/news/stories/andlinger (accessed August 20, 2009).

11. Mary E. Napier (senior research associate, DeSimone Research Group), in discussion with Goldstein, February 24, 2009.

12. Robert E. Litan, Lesa Mitchell, and E. J. Reedy, "Commercializing University Innovations: Alternative Approaches," May 16, 2007, http://papers.ssrn.com/sol3/papers.cfm?abstract_id=976005 (accessed August 20, 2009).

Chapter 3

1. Phillip Clay (chancellor, MIT), in discussion with Goldstein, November 20, 2008.

2. James Plummer (dean, School of Engineering, Stanford University), in discussion with Goldstein, November 15, 2008.

3. Deshpande Center website, "About the Center," http://web.mit.edu/deshpandecenter/about.html (accessed August 20, 2009).

4. Charles Cooney (Robert T. Haslam Professor of Chemical Engineering, Massachusetts Institute of Technology; faculty director, Deshpande Center for Technological Innovation), in discussion with Goldstein, February 18, 2009.

5. Ibid.

Chapter 4

1. Emily Eakin, "How to Save the World? Treat It Like a Business," *New York Times*, December 20, 2003.

2. Peter F. Drucker, *Innovation and Entrepreneurship: Practice and Principles* (New York: Harper Business, 1993), 23.

3. Robert A. Guth, "Bill Gates Issues Call for Kinder Capitalism," *Wall Street Journal*, January 24, 2008.

4. Skoll Foundation website, "About the Skoll Foundation," http://www.skollfoundation.org/aboutskoll/index.asp (accessed August 20, 2009).

5. Ibid.

6. Jeff Goodell, "The Guru of Google," *Rolling Stone*, April 17, 2008.

7. Michael Chu and Jean Steege Hazell, "The Omidyar-Tufts Microfinance Fund: Striving to Reshape the Social Enterprise Capital Markets," *Harvard Business Publishing Brief Cases*, October 20, 2007.

8. Ibid.

9. Ibid.

10. Lawrence Bacow (president, Tufts University), in discussion with Goldstein, June 27, 2008.

11. Joel Thomas and Sindhura Citineni (founders, Nourish International), in discussion with Goldstein, September 10, 2008.

Chapter 5

1. Werner Z. Hirsch and Luc E. Weber, eds., *As the Walls of Academia Are Tumbling Down* (London: Economica, 2002), 88.

2. Association of American Universities, "Report of the Interdisciplinarity Task Force," October 2005, 1.

3. Barbara Entwisle (director, Carolina Population Center, University of North Carolina at Chapel Hill), in discussion with the authors, June 12, 2008).

4. Association of American Universities, "Report of the Interdisciplinarity Task Force," 6.

5. Jim Spudich (cofounder and first director, Bio-X, Stanford University), in discussion with Goldstein, October 15, 2008.

6. Ibid.

7. Heideh Fattaey (director, Bio-X programs and operations), in discussion with Goldstein, October 15, 2008.

8. Carla Shatz (director, Bio-X; professor of biology and neurobiology, Stanford University), in discussion with Goldstein, November 20, 2008.

Chapter 6

1. Judith Rodin (former president, University of Pennsylvania; president, Rockefeller Foundation), in discussion with the authors, August 12, 2009.

2. Ibid.

3. Erskine Bowles (president, University of North Carolina), in discussion with the authors, November 20, 2008.

4. Ibid.

5. Ibid.

6. Adam Bryant, "Leadership without a Secret Code," *New York Times*, October 31, 2009.

7. John Hennessy (president, Stanford University), in discussion with the authors, April 20, 2009.

8. Ibid.

9. John Hennessy, "Innovation as the Crux of Entrepreneurship" (lecture at Stanford University's Entrepreneur's Corner, Stanford, Calif., February 18, 2009), http://ecorner.stanford.edu/authorMaterialInfo.html?mid=2111 (accessed September 1, 2009).

10. Hennessy discussion, April 20, 2009.

11. Hennessy, "Innovation as the Crux of Entrepreneurship."

12. Ibid.

Chapter 8

1. James Plummer (dean, School of Engineering, Stanford University), in discussion with Goldstein, November 15, 2008.

2. Audrey Williams June, "Presidents: Same Look, Different Decade," *Chronicle of Higher Education*, February 16, 2007.

3. College and University Professional Association for Human Resources, *2008–09 Administrative Compensation Study* (Knoxville, Tenn.: CUPA-HR, 2009).

4. Steven B. Sample, "Annual Address to the Faculty, 2008" (public address, University of Southern California, Los Angeles, February 2008), http://www.usc.edu/president/speeches/2008/faculty_address.html (accessed September 1, 2009).

5. "Long-Serving President of U. of Virginia Will Retire Next Year," *Chronicle of Higher Education*, June 12, 2009.

6. John Hennessy (president, Stanford University), in discussion with the authors, April 20, 2009.

Chapter 9

1. Peter F. Drucker, *Innovation and Entrepreneurship: Practice and Principles* (New York: Harper Business, 1993), 26.

2. William Baumol (professor of economics and academic director, Berkley Center for Entrepreneurship and Innovation, Stern School of Business, New York University), in discussion with the authors, June 18, 2008.

3. For more on the triple bottom line, see Stuart L. Hart and Mark B. Milstein, "Creating Sustainable Value," *Academy of Management Executive* 17, no. 2 (2003).

Chapter 11

1. Bill Gates, "2009 Annual Letter from Bill Gates," http://www.gatesfoundation.org/annual-letter/Documents/2009-bill-gates-annual-letter.pdf (accessed September 1, 2009), 2.

2. Ibid., 4.

3. Ibid., 6.

4. Ibid., 12.

5. Matthew Bishop and Michael Green, *Philanthro-Capitalism: How the Rich Can Save the World* (New York: Bloomsbury Press, 2008).

6. Joel L. Fleishman, *The Foundation: A Great American Secret: How Private Wealth Is Changing the World* (New York: PublicAffairs, 2007).

7. Stephanie Strom, "Alumni Group Tries to Elicit Social Action From Harvard," *New York Times*, June 3, 2008.

8. Greg Mitchell, "Study's Claim on the 'Myth' of Obama's Small Donor Base Is Itself a 'Myth,'" *Huffington Post*, November 29, 2008, http://www.huffingtonpost.com/greg-mitchell/study-that-hits-myth-of-o_b_147135.html (accessed September 1, 2009).

9. Kiva website, "Press Center, Latest Statistics," http://www.kiva.org/about/facts/#Stats (accessed September 1, 2009).

Conclusion

1. "Up Front: Drew Gilpin Faust," *New York Times*, September 6, 2009.

Engines Revisited—A Three-Year Tune-Up

1. On Bobby Allen's digital initiative, see Harry Lynch, "Bobby Allen's Life of Research Turns Digital," *Raleigh News and Observer*, August 12, 2012, http://www.newsobserver.com/2012/08/12/2263136/bobby-allens-life-of-research.html. For an example of a digital humanities approach in literary criticism, see Steve Lohr, "Dickens, Austen and Twain, Through a Digital Lens," *New York Times*, January 26, 2013, http://nyti.ms/VCwsWl.

2. See Jordan Weissman, "53% of Recent College Grads Are Jobless or Underemployed—How?," *The Atlantic*, April 23, 2012, http://www.theatlantic.com/business/archive/2012/04/53-of-recent-college-grads-are-jobless-or-underemployed-how/256237/.

ACKNOWLEDGMENTS

Of course we said yes when our friend and editor David Perry asked us to consider writing a book about innovation and entrepreneurship in the research university. Suffice it to say we didn't know exactly what we were getting into, and being entrepreneurs at heart we assumed it was just another problem to solve. Once the complexity of the task became clear, though, we did what we always do when faced with a difficult situation—ask for help. Fortunately, our friends and colleagues were ready and able.

Leslie Boney, Judith Cone, George Lensing, Will Baumol, and Deborah Hoover all read drafts of the manuscript from cover to cover and provided detailed and insightful comments that contributed substantially to the final product. Mary Napier read and helped shape the chapter on entrepreneurial science. John Stewart, Lowry Caudill, Julia Sprunt Grumbles, Jim Johnson, Emil Kang, Francesca Talenti, Kimberly Jenkins, and Kevin Fitzgerald all contributed to our thinking as we developed and taught courses in the minor in entrepreneurship at UNC. Our colleagues Bernadette Gray-Little, James Moeser, Jack Kasarda, Dick Krasno, Tom Kenan, Steve Jones, Tony Waldrop, Matt Kupec, Jamie May, and Doug Dibbert all offered advice and support over many years for the work that led to this book. Erskine Bowles not only provided an insightful interview that shaped our chapter on leadership but, by example, has taught us how entrepreneurial thinking can dramatically influence the trajectory of a great university system.

We are deeply indebted to those who allowed us to interview them and regret we could not include all of them in the final manuscript. Ruel Tyson, Jim Spudich, Phil Clay, John Hennessy, and Joe DeSimone gave us special insights that dramatically shaped our thinking. Special thanks go to David Burney for introducing us to the work of Roger Martin on organizational responsibility. Greg Dees provided important revisions to the chapter on social entrepreneurship. Jeff Timmons, who died before we began the book, started us along our path and suggested the magic that might be possible when entrepreneurship is added to the vast resources of a research university. Joel Fleishman provided deep insight for the chapter on the New Donors and support and enthusiasm throughout the project. Attempting to meet his high standards and expectations has been a singular challenge.

Joel Sutherland, one of our former students, and Clay Schossow, along with the students in our first-year seminar, built the website that we hope will allow conversation generated by this book to continue for some time to come. Nancy Kocher, Faye Lewis, Brenda Kirby, and Barbara Leonard provided invaluable administrative support, and Genny King provided important background research. Liz Gray served as a careful copyeditor and completed her work in a timely manner.

Bo Thorp, Clay Thorp, and Katherine and Max Goldstein have all made contributions too numerous to mention here.

We are deeply grateful to our editorial assistant, Jeff Canaday, who has been a critical partner throughout the process. He made substantial suggestions about the content of every chapter, as well as helping us with grammar and style. He worked nights and weekends to help us make deadlines, and he did all of this with grace and good humor.

Most important, we are greatly indebted to our students and colleagues and to all who have built and grown our own great university and our peer institutions throughout the nation and the world. It is a privilege to be part of this community and we hope our work will in some small way repay our debt of gratitude.

INDEX

CNBC, 155
Coleman, Mary Sue, 115
Columbia University, 34
Commercialization: and innovation, 3; relationship to entrepreneurship, 6, 7, 36, 136; potential for as funding criterion, 18, 19, 30, 31; and technology transfer, 24, 34, 35, 38–39, 159–61; and entrepreneurial science, 24–37 passim; and enterprise creation, 38–52 passim; and translational disciplines, 42–43, 99
Cooney, Charles, 47–49
Cornell, Ezra, 4
Cornell University, 4
Creativity: and research universities, 5, 84, 120, 136; and entrepreneurship, 6, 54, 84, 120; and solution of big problems, 10, 14, 20; and multidisciplinarity, 78, 84; and leadership, 86. *See also* Innovation
Crow, Michael, 69, 71–72
"Crowdsourcing," 15

Danon Yogurt Company, 57
Danone Group, 57
Darden, Tom, 57
"Dashboard." *See* Accountability: and metrics
Dees, Gregory, 55–56, 59
Democratic Party, 14
Department of Defense: Synergistic Idea Development Award, 19
DeSimone, Joe, 27–30, 33, 99
Digital humanities, 156
Donors, private: and university endowments, 3, 17, 62, 145–46, 147; problem-focused, results-based expectations of, 10, 17–18, 23–24, 69–70, 71, 142–50 passim; and

entrepreneurial science, 23–24; interdisciplinarity favored by, 31, 69–70, 75–76, 77, 109; and social entrepreneurship, 54, 57, 59, 60–64; engagement of, 60, 142–44, 148–49; and university leaders, 88–89; accountability to, 134; philanthro-capitalists as, 141, 142–47, 148–49; small, 141, 146–48, 149–50; new breed of, 141–50. *See also* Funding
Donors Choose, 147, 149
Drayton, Bill, 54, 58
Drucker, Peter, 3–4, 36, 55, 118, 123, 127
Duke University, 55–56, 59, 66, 76, 101, 146; business school, 61
DuPont, 28

eBay, 59, 60, 62, 127
Ehrman, Bart, 99
Elon University, 66
Emory University, 34
Engineering: and entrepreneurial science, 26, 34, 36; and enterprise creation, 39–50 passim; as translational discipline, 41–43, 99; and entrepreneurial skills/thinking, 44–45, 49, 120; within research universities, 46, 50, 111; and multidisciplinary centers, 49, 69–82 passim; and teaching entrepreneurship, 49–50, 59, 121, 126
Enron, 126
Entrepreneur(s): working in conjunction with academics, 4, 45, 48–49, 119, 121–23; as innovators, 5–6, 151–52; within research universities, 6, 36–37, 153–54; definition/attributes of, 6–7, 8, 19, 118–19, 135, 151, 152, 154; and

teaching entrepreneurship, 44, 48, 49–50, 51, 57, 103, 104–5, 118, 119, 121–23, 127–28; interaction with students, 44, 57, 128; social, 49–67; academic, 71–72, 76–78, 100–101; as new breed of donors, 141–50. *See also* Entrepreneurship/entrepreneurial thinking

Entrepreneurship/entrepreneurial thinking: as missing ingredient in universities' readiness to innovate to solve big problems, 5–6, 9, 20–21, 53, 58–59, 64, 151–54; within research universities, 6–8, 9–10, 20–21, 40, 50, 68, 94–95, 97–105 passim, 119, 120–21, 132, 153–54; relationship to business/commercialization, 6, 7, 23–24, 36; and problem solving, 7, 10, 11, 36, 50, 58–59, 68, 152–53; relationship to traditional academic disciplines, 7–8, 19, 71–72, 120, 155–57, 162; students and, 10, 15–16, 56–58, 64–67; and new information-based tools, 12–15; and individual, 13, 76–78, 84, 85; social, 15, 53–67, 101–2; and interdisciplinarity, 19, 68–84 passim, 153; and priorities of donors/funding sources, 23–24, 57–58, 59, 64, 141–50; teaching of, 36, 46–52, 59, 103, 118–32, 156–59; and enterprise creation, 38–52; and accountability/metrics, 64, 104, 133–40 passim. *See also* Entrepreneur(s); Leader(s)/leadership: entrepreneurial style of in research universities; Science, entrepreneurial

Entwisle, Barbara, 72, 74

Facebook, 16
Faust, Drew Gilpin, 90, 113, 151
Five Minds for the Future (Gardner), 19
Fleishman, Joel, 143, 144
Florida, Richard, 5
Fogelman, Kelly, 64–65
Folkman, Judah, 25
Foster, Norman, 78, 80
Foundation, The (Fleishman), 143
Foundations, private, 144–45. *See also* Donors, private; Funding
Fowler, Mayhew, 14
Funding: for solution of big problems, 11, 12, 23–24; for political campaigns, 14, 147; for entrepreneurial science, 22–24; for scientific research, 22–24, 30, 31, 33; for social entrepreneurship, 55, 58–59; for multidisciplinary centers, 69, 71, 74, 82–83, 112; for teaching entrepreneurship, 103; level of as measure of university success, 114
—sources of: problem-focused, results-based expectations of, 3, 17–18, 19, 23–24, 30, 33, 69, 71; state and federal government as, 3, 23, 69, 115, 134, 144, 151; traditional, decrease in, 10, 17, 134, 151; interdisciplinarity favored by, 31, 116–17; accountability to, 134

See also Donors, private

Gardner, Howard, 17
Gates, Bill, 23, 59; as new donor, 141, 142–43, 144, 145, 146. *See also* Bill and Melinda Gates Foundation
Gates, Melinda, 23. *See also* Bill and Melinda Gates Foundation
Gaudio, Bob, 157

neering, 41, 49, 50, 71, 93, 111; Business School, 46, 61, 132; Summer Institute for Entrepreneurship, 46–47; Stanford Technology Ventures Program (STVP), 49–50; Bio-X/Clark Center, 69, 70, 76, 78–79, 80–83, 101, 117

Starbucks, 125

Startup.com (film), 126

Stonyfield Farms, 57

Strategic planning, 51, 135–40

Students: and social networking, 10; and focus on problem solving, 10, 15, 16, 101–2, 109; and social entrepreneurship, 15, 56–58, 64–67, 132; millennial, and transformation of the academy, 15–16; idealism of, 16, 56, 57–58; as core of university, 32; and enterprise creation, 43–52 passim; teaching entrepreneurship to, 118–32, 156–59; job preparation of, 161–62

Symantec, 50

Teach for America (TFA), 16, 44, 56, 57

Tea Party movement, 14

Technology transfer, 24, 34–35, 39, 40; and standard licensing agreements, 159–61

Tenure, 41, 71, 72, 102, 106, 110–11

Texas Instruments, 43

Thomas, Joel, 66

Timmons, Jeffrey, 122

Translational disciplines, 40–52, 99

Tufts University: Omidyar-Tufts Microfinance Fund (OTMF), 61–63; Institute for Global Leadership, 63

Turner, Ted, 128

Twitter, 16

Tyson, Ruel, 76–78, 79, 80, 100–101, 148

U.S. Agency for International Development (USAID), 69

University Network for Social Entrepreneurship, 60

University of Berlin, 4

University of Bologna, 5

University of California, Berkeley: Haas School of Business, 49

University of California, San Diego: Center for Human Development, 69, 74

University of Chicago, 4

University of Florida, 34

University of Illinois: Beckman Institute, 74, 76

University of Michigan, 115

University of Minnesota, 18

University of North Carolina at Chapel Hill, 2, 102, 115, 146; DeSimone Research Group, 27–30, 33; teaching entrepreneurship at, 36, 66, 104–5, 118–32, 156–59; Carolina Challenge, 51; Office of Technology, 51; Kenan-Flagler Business School, 51, 148; Launching the Venture program, 51–52, 66; and social entrepreneurship, 56–57, 58, 64–67; Carolina Population Center, 69, 72, 74; Institute for the Arts and Humanities (IAH), 74, 76–78, 79, 80, 81, 148; School of Public Health, 74, 114, 148; Parr Center for Ethics, 148–49; and new donors, 148–50; Innovation Roadmap at, 155; Carolina Express License at, 159–61

University of North Carolina System, 87, 89

University of Padua, 152
University of Pennsylvania, 85, 88
University of Southern California, 115
University of Toronto: Rotman School of Management, 107
University of Virginia, 115
Ursinus College, 27–28

Venkataswamy, Govindappa, 125
Venturesome Economy, The (Bhide), 44
Virgin Airways, 60
Virginia Polytechnic Institute and State University (Virginia Tech), 28
Von Braun, Wernher, 11, 31

Webb, Jim, 31
Western Union, 4

"What Is Strategy?" (Porter), 124
White, Andrew D., 4
Whitehead, Alfred North, 151
Wikipedia, 13–14
wikis, 14
World Economic Forum, 60
World Health Organization, 64
World Lung Foundation, 64
World Wide Web. *See* Internet

Yahoo, 93
Yale University, 66
Young, Michael (Lord Young of Dartington), 54
YouTube, 14
Yunus, Muhammad, 54–55, 57, 61, 62